A 1950's Boy

Growing up in Swansea

MEMORIES

Introduction

At first

Going to school

Jack's House for tea

Tonsils op

Dressing up

Comics

The Second World War

Family

Stouthall

Reading

Dad's first car

Pets

Buses

Fires and Dramatic events

Holidays

Scouts

Playing

Games

Food

Television

The Sea

Church and Sunday School

Differences

Houses

Swansea

Postscript

End piece

Introduction

Early memories are usually deceptive. Do you really recall this moment in your life, all that time ago? Is it more likely to be a second hand story in which you have assumed the starring role after years of being told about it until you are now sure you remember it clearly. My earliest memories are an odd mixture of places, events and people. I have supplemented the stories with some original photos and despite some attempts at photo editing the low definition of many of them still retain the haziness and blur from all those years ago and maybe that is just as it should be so I make no apologies for this.
I should also say at this point that I am enormously grateful to my family and friends for giving me a very happy childhood. My parents I am sure gave me the best possible start in life that I could have wished for.

This series of my memories are not scrupulously organised although I have attempted some rudimentary sorting into themes but inevitably there is still some cross over. There is also the question of why write this stuff down? Is it merely nostalgia - understandable having attained the three score and ten in years or is it more than that. Clearly it isn't a case of fame with publishers and newspapers clamouring to get insights into my life and how my childhood made me the man I am today for I am not famous or even notorious and known only to my circle of friends and work mates etc that I have encountered through my life. If there is one single driver it may be that I have been looking back to remind myself of how life was different then and maybe how we struggle sometimes to understand or appreciate aspects of today's world. All things then were not better nor worse but many certainly were different.
Although I grew up in Wales I believe that many of the experiences would be common to people of a similar age in other parts of the country. I probably don't make very much of my Welshness at that time. The language wasn't heard very much in Swansea but was more prevalent in rural areas

and other parts of the principality, as I was to discover some years later at university in Aberystwyth.

Road signs and official documentation had yet to become bilingual. I wasn't aware of any Welsh language television in the 1950's. The Welsh assembly was some years in the future and there were no Welsh lessons in my junior school. When I went up to secondary school Welsh language lessons were limited to one a week in the first year (which the Welsh master used for an extensive post-mortem of the school's rugby first XV which was clearly his overriding passion.) Latin and French lessons took more time on the syllabus without any sports based digression. Perhaps the only indication that we were a Welsh grammar school was the singular existence of school rugby football teams and the total exclusion of soccer from organised games. To the extent that it was not unknown for a master to give a talking to a pupil 'rumoured to be playing for a soccer team' to seriously reconsider his chosen sport!

In conclusion it was possible to be less conscious of cultural differences and this may well have been compounded by my mother's English roots, the part of Wales we lived in and the lack of the language in our lives. At least we still had laverbread and welsh cakes, though not leeks due to my Dad's onion aversion. Like many others it took my move after university to live and work in England for me to more fully embrace 'the Land of my Father's.' I found that being Welsh gave one some latitude to think or see things differently, or at least a convenient excuse for doing so.

I recall now, with some horror and amusement, once sitting on an interview panel discussing a candidate that we had just seen when the colleague said, "Well he's very able and bright but he is Welsh !"

Somewhat shocked, I interrupted and said -

'David, just let me say…..'

David carried on -"Well, I know I am stereotyping but they can be prickly and argumentative…."

I tried again to interrupt-

'David, before you say any more...'

But he was on a roll - "Some of them just have a chip on their shoulder and go out of their way to ….."

I couldn't take any more -
I loudly shouted -'DAVID - I AM WELSH.'
Undaunted he answered -
"Good God, are you? It doesn't show."
Anyway, we gave Alun the job - and he could be difficult but not so much with me and we didn't refer David to the Race Relations Board, different times!

At First

One of my first memories has to be a street party for the coronation of Queen Elizabeth in the summer of 1953 when I would have been around two and three quarters. The sight of a row of tables in the street complete with table cloths would have been unusual enough to imprint itself on my memory. On the same day my father told me how he pushed me in my push chair down the middle of the main road which was empty of the usual traffic. I'm not sure that I have my own memory of this but now have an 'acquired' one through repeated tellings of the event. The only memory I have older than this was being taken to view what became our first family house in Tycoch Road, Swansea. My memory of this was that on the landing was a chest of drawers and on top of this was a large model ship, a fully rigged sailing galleon in a glass case. Then the even stronger memory was my bitter disappointment when on moving in day I ran upstairs to find that although the chest of drawers was still there the model ship had gone. I have now come to terms with the disappointment.

A later memory at the age of 3 years and one month was the arrival of my younger brother. I remember that I slept in the double bed with my Dad while my Mum was in hospital and each morning was given a small present, gift wrapped by my mother, to compensate for her absence. I can't actually remember her return with my baby brother, but was told that I welcomed him by emptying a handful of my toys into his pram and nearly smothering him. This could be interpreted as an act of generosity or a disguised assassination attempt.

When I was born it seemed that my parents lived in what was then called 'rooms' which I believe would today be called a flat in a house occupied by a landlady who owned the house. This was not an ideal arrangement for a young married couple with a new baby so we were to move in with my grandparents, my mother's parents and I was told we lived there until I was two and a half years old.

Understandably, because of my age my memory of this time is limited though I do have a few. One is of a basket full of tiny kittens in my grandmother's kitchen, although I don't remember them even having a cat. The other is of going to town with my mother to go to the market which wasn't the later covered one but was a temporary outdoor market. There were tarpaulin canopies like ones I have recently seen in Mediterranean street markets but here, no doubt to keep the rain off. On the return up the hill to Heathfield where my Grandparents lived I remember coming up stone steps with metal railings, one side topped with small coloured globes, like those on mid-century style coat hooks. I wonder if they are still there.

Going to School

My first day at school wasn't particularly traumatic as far as I can remember. It certainly wasn't much of a commute as we lived next door but one to the school itself and our neighbour was the school caretaker. The proximity had benefits later on when I could play after hours in the playground with friends. The school itself comprised two red brick buildings , single storey for the class rooms and school hall but I believe the were some offices on the first floor in a tower which I think was the head teacher's study. One building was for the infants and the second larger one for the junior school pupils.
My memory of the first day is being asked if I knew anyone

there and when I replied that I knew a larger dark haired boy, the son of one of the local shopkeepers that my Mum had arranged an unsuccessful play afternoon with some weeks earlier.
Although, I remember his name and encountered him later in grammar school I will preserve his anonymity as I feel its

too late to start a friendship. The details of why the chemistry was wrong are lost to me now but when I identified him the teacher asked me if I would like to sit with him. Rather confidently I said 'No.' So I started my education sitting in a double desk by myself. I like to think it was an early indication of my independent spirit which may also show that certain characteristics are formed early. I remember the desks being wooden with a fold up lid and a cast iron black metal frame that the hard wooden seats were attached to. The top surface had an inset groove to hold a pen or pencil and a hole for an inkwell although it was a number of years, I believe, before we were let loose with pen and ink after mastering pencils. I think we had the same style all through infants and junior school although would hope the size was increased in the later years to accommodate our young growing frames.

Our proximity to the school meant that I could walk to school by myself from a very early age. This was hardly a risk, as I said earlier, we lived next door but one to the school so front door to the school gate was a walk of twenty yards at most, all in my Mum's vision I guess.

This proved to me a disadvantage when in the top class at infants at the age of seven or so I was summoned to the headmistresse's study on the first day of term, somewhere I had studiously avoided until then. It was mid morning break and the friends I was playing with were as surprised as I was to be called out of the playground by a teacher to go to the Head. Once there I must have had a guilty expression but was quickly reassured.

"It's alright you are not in trouble." I was asked whether my younger brother had started in the school that morning which he had.

"Well, he's escaped and we hope he's gone home - please go and check and ask you mother if he can return. At home I found a very disgruntled four year old negotiating with my mother.

I caught -"Been to school, don't like it, DON'T LIKE IT!" I guess the two of us escorted him back under protest.

Ironically he went onto a career in education so I guess he revised his initial opinion.

I appear in the back row as the sixth boy from the left hand side. I do remember the names of some fellow classmates but will preserve their dignity. I will say that my friend Jack appears with improbably fair hair as the third boy from the right in the middle row and despite our better judgement he has given his permission to embarrass him with this exposure.

Jack's house for tea

One of my first memories of socialising outside the family was tea at the house of my first schoolfriend, Jack. We would have been four or five years old and details of the first of many visits to his house are sketchy but one detail that struck me at the time was when we went to watch children's hour on television in 'the front room.' The curtains were drawn, possibly to more easily see the faint, small grey picture in early televisions but it was a new experience for me as in daylight we watched television with the curtains open. I guess the experience prepared me for the later experience of going to the cinema or 'the pictures' as it was colloquially known at the time. More of the pictures later. Other memories with Jack included envying two impressive presents sent to him by a relative, possibly from abroad. The first was a large form of Swiss army penknife that came fully equipped with a spoon and fork and was much envied by me along with other members of the local cub pack we belonged to.

The other even more covetable gift was an actual working space rocket. This was used in the garden and was propelled by mixing water with some magical tablet, probably bicarbonate of soda. Then standing away and after a countdown pulling a string which removed a cap in the bottom of the bright red rocket between the tail fins thus allowing the rocket to spectacularly shoot high in the air. Unfortunately, living in the suburbs it inevitably landed in one of the neighbours' gardens and there was a negotiation process over whose turn it was to either sneak into the garden to retrieve it or more likely timidly knock on the neighbour's door to politely ask if we could retrieve it. Experience proved it was more acceptable to ask to retrieve our ball rather than admit to bombarding the neighbour with chemical weaponry, albeit of limited mass destruction capability. Use of the rocket was rationed partly by the limited supply of magic tablets but also by the limited patience of neighbours to incursions into their gardens.

As an adult I discovered a modern version using water, a plastic drink bottle and compressed air via a bike pump and I can heartily recommend it as a way of keeping me and Labrador retriever entertained. Thankfully my garden as an adult was large enough that I didn't need embarrassing encounters with neighbours - asking for my rocket back. We lost touch after going away to university but some twenty years later through our mothers we re-established contact so we are now able to regularly reminisce about those days. A few years back we met in Jack's Mum's house and the memories of those teas and playing in the garden came flooding back.

Tonsils op

One of my early traumatic memories was going to hospital around the age of seven for the removal of my tonsils. In the 1950's this seemed to be a rite of passage for many children though I haven't heard whether this continues in the 21st century. I presume modern day children have evolved to naturally destroy their own tonsils by the diligent consumption of massive quantities of crisps and junk food, (I must commission some research on this.)
I can clearly recall being at home packing a small case with pyjamas, dressing gown, some books and comics as well as my favourite 'teddy,' Jacko a yellow glove puppet monkey. The other prized possession put in the case was a recently acquired metal 'Dinky toy' a Gloster Javelin delta winged RAF model plane.
I don't remember the journey but I do recall the sense of loneliness being left in a ward with a number of other small boys, presumably all there for a similar procedure. I am not sure about the length of stay in the hospital but prior to my actual operation there was time to suffer further trauma when returning to the ward I discovered two similar looking boys in the next beds playing with a toy plane which after checking my case and bedside table found that my own precious plane was missing. An argument ensued culminating in my grabbing the plane back after punching the boy in the nose. I emphasise I was not normally given to violence but the distress of the strange surroundings compounded by my sense of injustice after the boy had insisted the toy had been 'loaned' to him by his twin brother. Two nurses restored peace and extracted a begrudged confession from the twin that I hadn't hit though it didn't bode well for a harmonious stay. It transpired that only one of the twins were there for surgery and the other one was bored and not sure why he needed to be there. Maybe that explained the theft but as is often the way in 'closed communities' the demonstration of strength meant that nobody messed with my stuff for the rest of the stay.
Fortunately I have no memory of the surgery but did become upset when waking with a sore throat after the anaesthetic

to discover that I had missed the ice cream that had been promised after surgery. This disaster was gleefully related by the twin boy in the next bed. I felt too frail and upset to punch him again. When I returned home I was alarmed when looking at my mouth to find what I had assumed were my tonsils was still present and could be seen hanging down at he top of my throat. To my later relief I discovered that this is the uvula and is not recommended for removal. So this ended my first solo encounter with the NHS. It did for some time make any viewing of the popular medical series on tv a less enjoyable experience than it might have been for me.

It is interesting what children envy in others and perhaps it comes from some inate desire for conformity or fitting in or maybe it is just the baser desire of pure envy and attention seeking. As a child, (and an adult) I have been fortunate enough so far to avoid breaking any of my bones and this is all the more surprising considering the dangerous childhood activities we engaged in that would be sure to fail any 21st century risk assessments. Maybe because of this I was always rather jealous when another child turned up at school with a limb or wrist in plaster and would for several days be the centre of attention with classmates autographing or drawing on the plaster cast.

The closest I came was spraining an ankle whilst at one of the bays in Gower on a summer evening's outing with the scout troop. I like to think I provided some useful real first aid and emergency practice after the hours we had spent in the cubs and scouts tying knots and practicing first aid treatments. I was carried up the cliff pathway several of the older scouts on some kind of improvised stretcher fashioned from poles and coats I think. An uncomfortable night with ice packs on the tender ankle and a visit to the local pharmacist who operated an informal medical triage service, (it avoided all those hours hanging about in the doctor's waiting room catching germs from all the sick people there - at least that seemed to be my Mum's theory.)

It was announced that I has a mild sprain and could go to school the next day wearing a modest elastic bandage that no-one autographed. The other thing we lived in dread of was appendicitis which the handful of children who had experienced an appendectomy would describe in gruesome detail including showing scars where they had been 'Cut Open!' Any rational examination of this would have concluded that the patient would be out cold and have little recollection of the treatment. Apparently one youngster had kept a piece of gauze bandage contains their seven stitches in black cotton and would proudly show this to everyone for the following twelve months.

In any event my only hospital visit for the removal of my tonsils had already done enough to deter any inclination for further visits to hospital.

Dressing up

It was a custom in schools in Wales that on St David's day children in the infants classes would come to school dressed in traditional costumes. This was easier for the girls with wool shawls and tall black hats but I have memory that around the age of six the favoured dress code for boys was as knights in armour. In those days there wasn't the availability of cheap supermarket costumes, well there weren't any supermarkets! It was creative home made costumes all the way. The cardboard helmet and wooden shield were within my parent's DIY capabilities but they really excelled themselves with the 'chain mail' jerkin created out of a sack with armholes and neck cut out and the whole ensemble painted with what must have been silver aluminium paint. I was very taken with it and set off the costume with grey balaclava, elastic snake belt, wellington boots and brandishing a plastic sword. Unfortunately the lateness of the preparations combined with the thickness of the paint on the sackcloth resulted in a certain sticky tackiness which no doubt left its mark in the school on chairs and elsewhere. I believe I was asked to go home to change at lunchtime.

Fancy dress was often considered to be part of Sunday school or cub group parties and as I said earlier these usually need to be fashioned form do-it -yourself materials. I was fortunate in having some relatives who lived abroad so there was more of a supply of exotic materials to choose from. Now in more culturally enlightened days some of this seems insensitive but the 1950's in Wales were limited in their diversity, and racial stereotypes were harvested from tv programmes, books and films. The perennial favourite was cowboy costumes given that any boy, and some girls were already owners of cowboy costumes and eager to brandish toy guns often equipped with loud percussion caps given any opportunity. I also remember my Mum creating a Davy Crocket hat out of some fur off cuts so that it had the requisite tail hanging down at the back. I don't think it was as popular with me as the more traditional cowboy hats as it was rather hot to wear but it proved useful to stop the family cat sleeping on my bed as when placed there he would leave the room quickly thinking a feline rival had already taken up residence.

The supply of a strange hat from Singapore twinned with a silk dressing gown and charcoal moustache and eyeliner plus a wool pigtail provided a Foo Man Choo costume similar to that of Tiger Lily's Dad in Rupert books. An even more exotic get up was seen in my African drummer boy outfit. One of my mother's older brothers was a captain in an African rifle regiment in what was then called East Africa. Souvenirs were either posted or brought home during leave periods. I remember a rather nonplussed postman delivering to us a whole coconut in its large hard outside husk with our address painted on it in yellow paint. Also my Dad trying several times to split it in the garden with a hatchet to extract the actual coconut. Of more use for fancy dress purposes was an African 'talking drum; which changed tone when the strings down the edge between the two ends were squeezed or relaxed under the arm whilst being hit with a strong bent drumstick which had been sent with it. Probably very annoying in the hands of any infant school child. I also believe looking at the photo that the bottom half of the outfit comprised of pieces of animal hide also posted from Africa and hopefully not part of some endangered species.

Some of, if not all of those, would be unacceptable today but those were different times!

Comics

An important part of our early literature were children's comics. The first one were more of the Janet and John variety and called Jack and Jill and the only characters I remember were Harold Hare and Dickie Dormouse (?) but I soon graduated to The Eagle comic with the wonderful cover story of Dan Dare - Pilot of the Future with his adventures in space. This was much more exciting and having obtained a reprint Christmas album book recently I realise how educational it was with detailed exploded technical drawings of ships, planes and power stations. Other educational articles would include advice on caring for pets and explanations, often complex in their detail, on topics such weather forecasting. In trying to jog distant memories of the contents I have retrieved the Eagle annual reprint that I bought relatively recently.

It's contents are quite a revelation, firstly there are adverts for sweets and toys which isn't so surprising but also ads for raincoats, boys shirts and hair brushes! There were also career based propaganda such as the joys of a career as a Civil Engineer and a detailed description of weather forecasting that a comprehensive absorption of would easily get a senior appointment on the TV weather staff, assuming you could also do the elaborate hand jive moves that now seem to be the most critical qualification!

I vaguely recall there were competitions and think I did once submit a coloured drawing into one, unsuccessfully. More revelatory are reprinted articles such as "I became a Knife thrower's target'" by Eagle Special Investigator, the late Macdonald Hastings, (I am joking about the late, as he obviously survived to tell the tale.) He was also, reluctantly, I should think, the author of the memorable "I became a Living Firework" in an asbestos suit !

Other encouragements to dangerous pursuits included ads for air rifles, catapults and boomerangs plus "use a pin to discover where you feel pain" in a science snippet. Another page shows instructions on dismantling a household tap to replace the washer and stop it dripping ! I am pretty sure I did not spend my childhood being bothered by dripping taps but can see that a more neurotic and organised child would find this appealing. Possibly one already seduced by the idea of a career as a civil engineer and now anxious to acquire useful skills in that area.

A reprint that would certainly catch the eye of an inquisitive boy is a short article entitled -

"Man About the House - Smashed the Crockery? Then mend it!"

With elaborate descriptions of glueing together broken shards and supporting them with string tourniquets....now this is all very well but call me suspicious - The title is not 'Smashed Crockery' but "Smashed the Crockery" which implies some active participation in the damage. I can just imagine little Johnnie left to his own devices on a wet afternoon in the dining room, next to the dresser with the priceless family china heirlooms, mother out of sight upstairs engaged in some household chore, a thought comes to him - "What was that intriguing article in my Eagle comic this week?" I think you can see the temptation.

Given a clearly over developed confidence by the publishers in the ability of their young readers to use prudence in copying such exhortations to living dangerously it is no surprise that one edition carried an explanation of of how the inclusion of advertisement subsidised the cover price. A clear indication that the 1 million or so young weekly readers were a highly sophisticated bunch and would appreciate such gems of modern finance in amongst the daring tales of Space, Scotland yard and the French Foreign Legion.

I do clearly remember my sense of acquisitiveness being stimulated by two such ads. The first was a Dan Dare radio station complete with two walkie talkies, impressive dials and buttons and a rotating searchlight? The console was topped with two impressive antennas like two miniature electricity pylons and was set up for morse code or voice communication. I don't recall the price but suspect it was beyond several months saving of pocket monies and perhaps the ad was not featured around the autumn when birthday or Christmas presents could be deployed. I was never to own one and although years later I saw one in an antique shop it seemed a lot to pay for a plastic box with a few lights and there was no certainty that it was capable of interplanetary communication. I have since discovered through a reminiscences with an old school friend that he still has one in his loft -"get that set on eBay, Cledwyn -liquidate the asset before its too late!"

I did at one time have sufficient funds to send away for another wonder of modern technology - a microscope that displayed images on a screen!

The 13/6 or whatever was duly sent off probably in postal orders and stamps and I ambushed the post man for several weeks despite reminders that the ad said "despatch may take up to 28 days." No amount of argument with my Mum about the detail of these terms would persuade me that the arrival of this wonder of technology wasn't imminent. Unfortunately when the long awaited device arrived, one day when I was at school, the house had to be scoured for the right batteries, two large ones possible from the doorbell or my Dad's torch, it proved a little disappointing.

Firstly the light thrown through a mirror onto the screen was rather dim, even in a darkened room. The image was pretty grainy and it seemed less powerful than my original microscope powered by sunlight which I had rashly passed on to my little brother declaring it as redundant technology. I don't think it lasted any longer than the one set of batteries and the novelty of seeing water fleas in pond water or the blurred hairs on the leg of a dead fly wore off pretty quickly. I was not destined for a career in science. But had learned a costly lesson on the power of advertising. There was also a blatant object lesson on the sins employed by advertisers in those faraway days. A full page picture shows an ecstatic boy sitting in a racing car some six foot in length brandishing a packet of Sugar Puffs bearing the slogan FREE INSIDE ! Model Racing Car. Described in the text as "Looking like the real thing." In the corner of the page was a much smaller picture with a caption of single coloured plastic cars which experience will teach you that is what you get. But it sees rather unfair to expect the average ambitious and optimistic eight or nine year old to expect this crappy piece of plastic in lieu of the full size car his contemporary is shown sitting in.

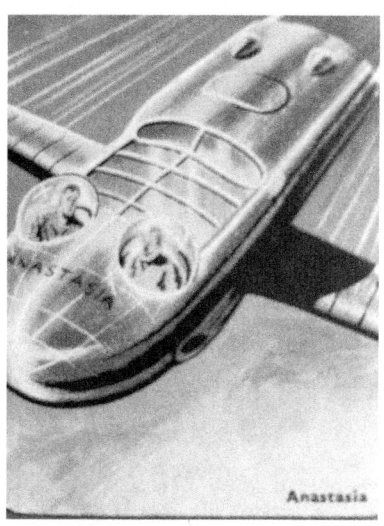
Anastasia

Never mind the question of how the car would be fitted inside the cereal box, (and still allow some room at least for some sugar puffs!) This was the era of nuclear power and sputniks in space and chocolates advertised with less fattening centres! A certain amount of gullibility was to be expected. The comic also carried hints on building your own spaceport using biro tubes and discarded tins and cardboard tubes but my artistic abilities or lack of patience didn't match the picture in the comic when it was finished and these attempts were soon abandoned.

The Eagle comic was unknowingly particularly formative for me in an unexpected direction. It was the first place in one of their 'history' articles that I learnt several facts about the island of Crete. Fact one, it was occupied in the second world war by the German army in the first mass attack by paratroopers. Secondly, the ancient palace at Knossos was unearthed by the British archeologist Arthur Evans and he named the civilisation the Minoans after the greek legend of the Minotaur and the maze.
These were the only two things I knew about Crete when many years later research for a summer holiday came up with Crete as a destination. It was such a successful holiday that we returned on a number of occasions, eventually buying a small stone village house for renovation as our

holiday home. The story of that adventure is told in my book for sale on Amazon -"A Small House in Crete." A further rather spooky coincidence is that the previous occupant of the house was named Anastasia - also the name of Dan Dare's spaceship - so the Eagle comic has been truly influential in my life. (Also proof that the early lesson in the power of subtle or otherwise advertising was not lost on me.)

A recent obituary this autumn recorded the passing at the age of 94 of one of the original illustrators of the Eagle comic, a lady called Greta Tomlinson who was reputed to be the inspiration for Professor Jocelyn Peabody first appearing in the fifth Dan Dare story and subsequently making regular appearances in the comic and providing a useful female role model for girls to follow science studies in those less egalitarian times.

There were other comics available but these were usually seen in friend's houses or waiting rooms. I think there was also a supply in junior school for 'wet play' days - relatively frequent in South Wales. The favourites were the Beano and the Dandy, arguably less intellectual than the Eagle comic but containing stories of the adventures of giants of children's literature such as Dennis the Menace, Beryl the

Peril, Roger the Dodger and the less poetic Lord Snooty and the Bash Street Gang or Corky the Kat!
I still think of Dennis's beloved shaggy dog Gnasher when I see a particularly black hairy dog and can only just resist asking the owner if it's called Gnasher. You have to take your fun where you can get it.

The Second World War

Though old enough to qualify as vulnerable through age during the recent pandemic and subsequent vaccination programme I am not old enough to have first hand knowledge of the second world war. But the dramatic events were recent and traumatic enough to form part of society's collective conscience in my early years.
The comics contained war stories and glowing tributes to Winston Churchill and the likes of national heroes such as Douglas Bader and Field Marshall Montgomery. It must be remembered that by the time I had acquired conscious memory, say the mid nineteen fifties, wartime was just a decade away. So it was similar to the time span since the 2012 London Olympics or the Banking Crash, events of much less significance in the public experience. It was not surprising that wartime stories were common currency for fifties conversation and events were often described as 'before the war' or 'in wartime.'
There was also tangible evidence all around, bomb sites where there were sometimes gaps in terraces of houses or large inexplicable craters now filled with brambles and buddleia plants. School playgrounds still contained air raid shelters and there were roadside concrete pill boxes and tank traps.
Undoubtedly it was a once in a generation collective trauma so it shouldn't be surprising that wartime cast such a long shadow and strongly figured in comics, films and childhood games as well as adult conversations which we would eagerly overhear.
It was also quite common for pieces of discarded military hardware to be used as playthings. Smelly rubbery gas masks, thankfully with the asbestos filters removed - usually - these were dangerous times. Also military binoculars, compasses and even bayonets and knives. I was the proud owner of my grand-dad's Air Raid Warden's tin helmet with ARP stencilled in white paint on the front. Unfortunately it was so large and heavy for my small young head and neck that it only had a ceremonial purpose and wearing for any length of time gave a very sore neck and it's looseness and

heavy weight made it impractical for any active boyhood re-enactments. More useful were an impressive large metal compass which had a lid that contained a sighting device and my brother shared with me a pair of powerful army issue binoculars that had been split to give us a monocular each. Any such collections were trumped in magnificent fashion during a visit to a schoolfriend's house where he showed me the play den he had at the bottom of his garden that he had with his brother. A Messerschmitt fighter cockpit cover in metal and glass! Ideal for battle of Britain play - where the hell did they get that? I later became aware of the German 'bubble cars' one of which was a Messerschmitt so it was more likely the cover was from the car as it was made by the same company but it was a dangerous time so who knows.

Family

I have mentioned my family and certainly in childhood they assume a great importance during your early years. My mother's family seemed to have military background and although I haven't indulged in the tracing my ancestors activities there are details that I remember from being told first hand by my parents. My mother was born in Chatham, Kent but that seemed almost coincidental as my grand father was a regimental Sergeant Major in the Royal Engineers and I believe that is where the family was stationed at that time,

January 1922. My grandfather had been born in Cardiff but I believe my grandmother was from Devon. Mum was the youngest of five along with her twin brother Douglas. The small photo here shows them seated on the left with one of my Mum's elder brothers as a baby. I believe she is yet to be born and the others in the photo are a mystery to me. Their surname was Gale and not long after her birth the family was part of the Royal Engineers garrison on the island

of Jamaica in the Caribbean where they stayed for the late 1920's and early 1930's. They came back to Britain for the twin's secondary education. Photos of that time show an idyllic childhood with palm trees, verandas in the sun and pony riding. There is a photo of the family with a car, captioned 'our Ford' and they seemed to have owned a number of horses. I am told that the life of a Regimental Sargeant Major would be relatively privileged and the photos seem to confirm this. Certainly their standard of living would be more comfortable than they would have enjoyed in 1920's Britain. The photo album suggests they were living near Newcastle in the Blue Mountains some 15 miles from

Kingston the capital, although Cedar Valley is also a caption

on some photos. This is described as being a British military post from 1840 to 1959. The location in a mountain area was a defence against yellow fever that had previously been a serious problem to garrisons stationed in Jamaica. It must have been quite adventurous for my grandparents to decide to take their young family there

My Mum was aways pleased if we spotted a mango or avocado at the greengrocers (a relative rarity in Wales in the 1950's,) and made us jealous talking of sugar canes and pineapples in their garden. Fortunately my Mum kept the family photo album of their time their and a fascinating record it makes. It must have been great childhood experience and the photos record the family in Havana as well as their time in Jamaica. The time in Jamaica must have been close to idyllic for my Mum at a young age with four brothers as company and horses, puppies and the sun and sea. She always spoke fondly about her happy memories of

their time there. Certainly the photos show them all enjoying themselves and it must have been quite an adaption returning to England in the depressed 1930's leading up to the war years.

I am hazy about the time-scale and my Mum talked of living in Abercynon back in Wales although photos show her in a Barrs Hill (Coventry), girls grammar school uniform and I know the family lived in Coventry during the war when my Grandad had the unenviable task of an air raid warden. She also talked of bringing a parrot back with them from Jamaica and the photo of my grannie with one confirms the story. The parrot was called Polly and later reminiscences will confirm a theme.

My Mum saw wartime service in the WAAF, (the women's service of the R.A.F.) and was a non-commissioned officer- a corporal, serving from September 1941 to March 1946. Sadly I don't recall many details about what Mum told me about her wartime service or possibly like many children I didn't pay much attention to her telling of it. I do remember her complaining that she wasn't eligible for a more adventurous overseas posting because she already had her four brothers serving overseas. She mentioned being stationed in Gloucester and possibly St Athen. Her RAF Service and Release Book contains some interesting details such as the page mentioning the return and disposal of the W.A.AF greatcoat and the fact that the princely sum of £1/10/0 would be received in return. There is also a section showing a stamp for encashment of postal drafts for a clothing allowance for the amount of £12 10 shillings.
There are details of a travel warrant and a stamp for food rations after leaving the service which sees to suggest she travelled from Birmingham to Neath. I know she was living in Neath with my grandparents after the war and I have a reference letter stating that she left employment at the Town Clerk's Office in February 1949 after getting married a year earlier and moving to Swansea with my Dad. It is like piecing together a jigsaw puzzle of connected parts of my parent's past.

To some extent my father's earlier life is a little clearer as it was all spent until he left school in the town of Swansea. I know he grew up in a house in the Uplands in Swansea, the same house that my grandparents were living in after I was born and used to visit them there.

He was one of three children having an older brother and sister. His father, Bob is described as a salesman on my parents marriage certificate and I believed he worked at the large Swansea department store of Ben Evans which was destroyed by bombing in the war. I know little of my Dad's

school days although he went to a secondary school not grammar school and was in the Swansea Sea scouts and left school at the age of fourteen and joined the merchant navy.

He later worked as an office boy in the local newspaper offices. After wartime service he returned to Swansea and worked in the costing office of Unit Superheaters works on the Strand and I remember talk of jobs being held open after the interlude of wartime service for this fortunate enough to safely return to them. While I was young Dad studied at

ROYAL ARMY SERVICE CORPS: Former members of the 36 Company, Swansea, last night held their first annual dinner at the White Swan Hotel, Swansea. All are ex-Eighth Army men and many Dunkirk veterans.

night school, qualifying as a chartered Company Secretary,

making up for his lack of earlier education.
I am trying to reconstruct those years along with my memories of Dad mentioning going to South America and the Cape in South Africa before the war. Wartime service must have been traumatic with being evacuated from the beach at Dunkirk then being deployed in Egypt and North Africa. Then the campaign through Italy was followed by a time in the occupying army in Palestine. Sadly, I have no comprehensive record of any of this, only some photo albums and collections of postcards. I know that after joining up and being posted to France it was not until 1946, some six years later, that he returned to a Swansea that he did not recognise with the town centre having being largely destroyed by German bombing. Coming out of the railway station he completely lost his bearings as he could see St Mary's church to the south when it should have been obscured by the large buildings of Ben Evans department store. He was confused as to which direction to take to get to the Uplands because of the radically changed landscape.
I guess that the extent of the damage from the bombing had been kept from family members serving overseas either out

of a need to hide bad news at home or due to strict censorship in wartime. I do remember being told that my parents met in a dance studio in Walter's Road having dancing lessons. Presumably my Mum having come from Neath and my Dad now back at work in Swansea. They were married on March 27th 1948 in the church of St David in Neath.
I waited for the 1950's to begin before I joined them in the world.

Stouthall

I was told by my parents that I was born in Gower and my birth certificate confirms this. In the years after the war a large house in its spacious grounds off the south Gower road

towards Port Eynon was used as a maternity ward perhaps as an overflow to Swansea's hospital in the town centre and of personal significance as the site of my tonsil removal! Stouthall was some 15 miles from the town and my parents home and my Dad said the bus ride of almost an hour down dark country lanes for the evening visiting hours was quite an ordeal though I think I am absolved of any blame for this. Car trips into Gower in adult life were often punctuated with my comment of "see that house," pointing through a gateway at a gloomy distant building down a drive and surrounded by tall trees full of crows -
"I was born there!"
It was once pointed out to me that I remain remarkably cheerful after such an unpromising start.
In recent years upon returning to live again in Wales, after a long absence, I had the opportunity to return to my actual birthplace. Unbeknown to me, my wife had found out that

although the house and grounds were now an outward bound style education centre they had started 'pop-up' restaurant bookings when the centre was not being used by students. So an autumn evening found me being driven out to supper in a mystery destination in Gower. As I had not heard of the occasional restaurant facilities I was mildly surprised to be driven through the entrance gates and up the drive to a house that I had left at a very tender age some sixty plus years earlier never anticipating to return. We were welcomed in a large reception hall with a stone floor and a sweeping steep curving staircase to the floors above. The owner led us through to a room he described as the library and offered us a welcoming drink and went away to bring menus for us. On his return he explained that the chef and kitchen staff normally catered for large student parties with hearty food after vigorous outdoor activities such as surfing, orienteering and sea kayaking etc. The chef had recently offered to do some small evening dinner parties with a more adventurous menu than his usual fare. Certainly the menu reflected this with local seafood dishes and Gower vegetables but my appetite wetting was interrupted by the question - "Have you been to Stouthall before?"

When I explained the background to my only previous visit he got quite animated and explained that earlier in the year they had entertained a party of retired nurses and midwives who had been able to describe how the house was set up when it was a maternity hospital. Then the shock question - "Would you like to see the room you were born in?"

Whilst not actually being sure that I did, nevertheless I found us following him up the staircase and going through a doorway off the long corridor landing into a small room with a set of bunk beds.

"The retired nurses told me this was the birthing room." he stated impassively. I was feeling more emotional although I wasn't really sure why. After a short silent contemplation and perhaps sensing a certain unease, at least on my part. He led us down the corridor and explained the larger ward room had been subdivided in later years but at the time of my arrival there would be a ward of a dozen or more beds where the mothers would spend up to a week before being allowed home. As we made our way down the steep staircase he relayed a final disturbing fact that in those days new mums were discouraged from too much exertion so the mother would be wheeled down the staircase in a wheel chair holding the new born on their lap. Looking at the precipitous stairs and the hard hall floor I concluded that I had been lucky to make it safely out of there.

Somewhat chastened we went into the dining room and enjoyed an excellent dinner. At least my appetite hadn't suffered.

Proof I got out of Stouthall and safely home.

Reading

I have always been a keen reader both for pleasure and out of necessity in later life but the reading habit was formed earlier through my enlightened parents. Some ten minutes from our house was the local Sketty library and although I can't precisely date my joining date I do remember sitting in the tiny chairs in the junior section trying to read a couple of books in addition to those I had quickly chosen to take home.

The library was supervised by a kindly bespectacled lady called Miss Finch and there was a bright, intelligent bird-like quality about her. I think that the last time I used the library would have been in the mid 1960's with my friend Robert who lived near me and we were studying similar GCE O level subjects and we would occasionally work there together on homework after school at the age of fourteen or so.

In recent years some fifty years later I attended a half day adult education course and to my amazement the library had hardly changed. I was pleased to see a framed picture on the wall of Miss Finch who had apparently continued working there for many decades.

The library was part of a sense of freedom as I only had to cross one side road to get to it so I was allowed to go there by myself from the age of eight or nine. The amount of freedom allowed to children in the 50's was a great contrast to more recent times.

I think early favourites for me among the books were Ladybird and Rupert books.

Many years later as an adult we lived in a house in the East Sussex high Weald with far reaching views over fields and woodlands to the South Downs. The view seemed strangely familiar and one day in a second hand bookshop I picked up an original Rupert book and flicking the pages I came across an illustration that virtually mirrored the view. Alfred Bestall the illustrator for the editions I would have seen at that time was often asked where Rupert's home village of Nutwood was supposed to be located, and told his first biographer "it is an amalgam of the scenery in the Weald, the wooded plateau of Kent and Sussex between the North and South Downs."

I wonder now whether the choice of our home with the views of the downs had been subconsciously influenced by

my early reading.
I quickly graduated to the Enid Blyton Famous Five and Adventure series but my all time favourite was the Just William books written by Richmal Cromton and these stories have aged well and I still occasionally listen to the audio books read by Martin Jarvis, the stories though of their time, have aged well.
What does surprise me is that the stories originally written in the 1920's and 30's echoed the life of children in the post war years. I believe I must have ignored the aspects of home life that were abnormal to my own with the Brown family having a cook and maid which was completely outside my experience. What did stay with me was an early experience of outrage expressed by a righteous juvenile on

the gross unfairness of adult behaviour towards a child who believed they were doing the right thing.

I have two personal examples that would both have made material for Just William plots. In homage to William and with apologies to Richmal Crompton I have written them as William stories.

Story 1 - The Burglary

It was the summer holidays and William had met up with his three friends who called themselves the Outlaws and gone to the local park. They were several weeks into the long summer holidays and had exhausted much of their usual activities. The morning had seen them unsuccessfully trying to catch fish in the park pond using a net crafted from a long stick, a wire hoop and a plastic bag. They had scared the ducks away during this process which prevented another favourite game of throwing small mud balls for the ducks who were convinced they were being fed. They were now looking wistfully up into the large horse-chestnut trees -"It's too early for conkers - I dunno why they have to wait until after the end of the summer holidays to have their conkers. It strikes me that it wud' have been fairer for the conkers to be ready in the holidays. It strikes me that this is just set up so we can only play conkers in school time when the rotten 'ole teachers are quick enough to confiscate them off us. It jus' strikes me that it's not fair." He said with a finality.
There was no argument to this from the other three outlaws who on many matters deferred to their self appointed leader. Ginger said, "It's not just collecting the conkers - there's the skill of knocking them out of the tree - an' I don't see why the rotten 'ole parkie has to chase us off. I ask you - why do they grow conker trees in the park if they don't want people to collect them. If we didn't collect them then the conkers would fill the park - I think you wouldn't be able to move in the park for conker trees. I think we are doing them a jolly good favour in collecting the conkers and stopping them filling up the park with conker trees. He was warming to his theme and was only interrupted by Douglas who said "And they say us throwing sticks to knock them down gonna damage the trees." William rejoined the dialogue to say "I jus' don't see how a stick can damage a tree - aren't trees made of sticks? If you want to break window you have to use something harder like a stone or a cricket ball."
Demonstrating a certain knowledge on the subject which was readily met with nods of agreement by his three friends who were also experienced in such matters.

"Anyway, said Ginger there aren't any conkers so what are we going to do?"

"What about hide and seek " suggested Henry who had been thinking about the last game of cricket that had involved glass breakage and the suspension of several weeks pocket money to pay for the repairs to his neighbours greenhouse. His pocket money was due to restart the following weekend and he had spent the last four weeks in its suspension planning the things he would buy once he was solvent again. The other three, in the absence of any immediate alternatives, agreed and William said"but it's only fair that you are It to begin with as it's your idea. Close your eyes, count to fifty an' we'll hide - an' no peeking."

With that the three friends scattered in different directions with Henry having leant against the nearest tree, eyes tightly screwed shut, and breathlessly counting to fifty as fast as he could.

'Forty -eight, Forty-nine, an' FIFTY," he cried. The other three in their hiding places behind a tree trunk, a low wall and a large dense shrub respectively were surprised to not hear the thunder of their friend's feet to follow the end of the countdown. Henry blinked his eyes to adjust to their short period of temporary blackness, then blinked again as he stared at the ground in front of him and not believing what he was seeing he loudly cried out. "Hey, you lot, come out - NOW!"

There was a series of muffled cries from different directions accusing that they were not falling for some dirty trick and Henry should continue the agreed game.

The repeated cry from Henry - "No really, it's no joke - come and see this."

There was something in the tone of Henry's voice that inspired William to be the first to emerge slowly from his hiding place to be followed by Ginger and Douglas, the latter still holding two small shrub branches as part of his improvised camouflage. The three friends reluctantly gathered around Henry with William muttering sarcastically "If you hadn't have wanted to play this game you shouldn't have suggested it -s'just not …." his voice tailed off as his gaze followed that of the the other two who were mirroring Henry as they all stared at the ground.

In the grass at their feet there was the a collection of shiny objects reflecting the summer sunshine.

William was the first to break the silence. " Cripes! I mean Crickey, where did you get this - there must be ….well there must be…more than.. I mean, looks like pounds!"

Bending down they picked up a collection of silver coins from the ground - shillings, sixpences, two shilling bits and even half crowns, the largest coin. While they pooled the handfuls on a patch of earth Douglas who had moved a few feet away from the other exclaimed - "Crumbs, there's more up here and a ten shilling note!"

Over the next quarter of an hour the ground all around was scoured by the outlaws with the four of them finally sitting on the ground at the top of a slope where a rough path ended at a solid door in a tall stone wall. They knew a large house lay behind it but in the past the park itself had provided sufficient entertainment and access into the house grounds was restricted by the locked gate in the wall and closed high wrought iron gates on the driveway. The search had culminated in finding two one pound notes and a blue five pound note just outside the gate. The total was estimated at over ten pounds a sum whose accuracy could not exactly be agreed on due to the four of them counting at the same time but not at the same speed.

"You made me lose my thread then," said Ginger angrily-" I was almost finished."

But together they unanimously agreed it was more money than they had individually or collectively had in their possession so the next task was what to do about it. Despite their various scrapes and adventures and their self-christened name the Outlaws were basically law abiding even if their own interpretation of the law was occasionally at odds with the rest of society. In fact they could be described as having something of an overdeveloped sense of justice.

'We have to find out who stole it," said William adopting his frequently assumed detective persona -"there must have been robbery, this is 'probly' just part of a huge haul by a

gang of desperate criminals - there's bound to be a reward for their capture - 'probly' even more than wots here!"
The thought of even greater riches certainly appealed to all of them and to have a role, certain to be a key one, in solving such a huge crime had even greater appeal. This was proving to be a great adventure.
Henry who was looking forward to possessing funds now proving to be over and above his reinstated meagre weeks pocket money confidently spoke up.
"We need to take it to the police station, they will properly record it, then catch the criminals and arrange out rewards."
"There'll likely be medals as well and stories put in all the newspapers we'll be in our parents good books for ever!" Ginger confidently asserted.
"Right, we'll go straight to the police station before the thieves return looking for what they've dropped.
If they're quick they can come here and take fingerprints and shoe prints- they could catch them later today I 'shud' think.
So gathering up the hoard of riches in Wiliam's handkerchief the happy band made their way out of the park and up the road to the local police station.
Arriving at the small local police station William led his band up the steps and into the station where all four stood in front of a high desk and decisively rang the large brass desk bell - three times.
A large uniformed man in a sergeants uniform came out of a back room and placing his large hands across the width of the desk and looked down at the assembled gathering.
"Yes boys" he said genially "what is it today- a major crime to report?"
William was impressed - "Yes, how did you know?
Have you caught them already?"
Henry couldn't wait -"Show him what we found - William."
So needing no further encouragement William noisily and proudly swung his handkerchief up onto the counter. The move opened the loose knot and dozens of coins spilled across the counter much to the surprise of the sergeant.
Quickly composing himself he spoke in a more businesslike voice.

"You'd better tell me all about this- how exactly did you come by this and where. I need all the details."
William replied in his own businesslike voice -
"Of course - you'll need to be catchin' em and want all our addresses to be sending the rewards an' medals and such."
Well we'll have to see about all that." said the officer as he opened a large journal and licked the end of his pencil.
But he did admit somewhat reluctantly that there had been a report of a local break-in the previous night but did not elaborate further. He also went so far to praise the boys for doing the right thing but then appeared anxious to terminate the interview and get on with other matters, possibly including quietly sitting down with a cup of tea.
It was some twenty minutes later that the outlaws left the police station and made their way home still in a state of mutual excitement about the days events. "Cor - wait till we tell our families about all this - an' the rewards and medals."
The excitement was short lived as William was quickly stopped in his attempt to tell of the events to his family who were already sitting down at the tea table by instructions to take of his outside shoes that were likely to be wet and muddy, they usually were, and to go and wash his hands.
Upon turning and trying to explain why he was late - he was interrupted again to be told to stop fabricating outlandish excuses for his lateness and to eat his tea which was getting cold. So that's what he did, the adventure had made him hungry but as he ate he was muttering and thinking how the lavish reward and recognition in the local press and possibly further afield would make them listen to him in the future.
Getting from the table and quickly leaving the room before he could be recruited into washing up he was heard to say with a tone of mystery -"You see - jus' you wait an' see..."
Unfortunately the coming weeks were to prove disappointing to the outlaws. Despite taking an unusual degree of interest in any post arriving at their houses and seizing the local evening paper from the delivery boy at the gate much to their parent's annoyance no acknowledgement of their efforts or the crime was publicised.

It was even suggested by William that whoever had coined the expression 'honesty was the best policy' had not experienced any involvement with their local police station.

I hope you agree this would make a suitable plot for a William tale and our indignation closely matched The emotions of the outlaws in their brushes with the vagaries of the adult world.

The second episode, although different in detail served to reinforce the gulf between our world and the adult one. It is based on a real event of the 1962 big freeze. Again I am imagining the story as it would be experienced by William and the Outlaws.

A Find

The winter was extraordinary! It had started snowing on boxing day and the return to school was put off as the plumbing had all frozen in the school. This was not as welcome to parents but was embraced joyously by most pupils in particular by William and his friends. Roads were blocked, ponds were frozen over with thick ice, even parts of the sea in the bay had ice and every day brought fresh falls of snow with opportunities for snowball fights and sledging. To the outlaws it was a dream come true. This was less fortunate for their mothers as each day brought fresh supplies of clothes to be washed and dried but such worries were outside the concerns of William and his friends. There were even some limited opportunities for adding to pocket monies with the occasional tips received from the grateful and rare stranded motorist needing pushing on the icy roads or out of a snowdrift.

"I'm fed up of pushing cars," said William glumly.

"An' they don't always give us money - they sometimes jus' drive off and shoot mucky snow all over us." replied Ginger just as gloomily.

"An' that one that drove up the pavement and into the bench wasn't half mad with us - as if it was our fault he didn't shout stop." complained Henry.

"S'not our fault if we can't see from the back - he was s'posed to be steerin' or brakin' or whatever he didn't do - s'hardly our fault - jolly ungrateful if you ask me. At least he was out of the way on the pavement an' the road and the pavement all jolly well look the same in the snow"

"I vote we give it a rest today and do summin' different." Douglas keenly agreed -"My Mum says I'll have to stay in for the week if I come home all wet again as I've no more dry clothes!"

They all agreed that their constant snow based activities were causing some laundry crisis at home and probably this was a conflict to be avoided -even temporarily.

"We cun go to the park there'll bound to be summin' to do there an' the ole parkie probly won't wanna chase us in the snow or be able to catch us if he did!"

It was decided, the park it was, so trudging through the snowy village streets and studiously avoiding stuck cars they set off, intent on their destination.

The park was a winter wonderland, the grassy banks thick with drifted snow and the trees bending under the weight of their icy loads. A detour off the path to throw snow balls up into the trees succeeding in dislodging substantial quantities of snow on the ground and similar amount on the outlaws themselves.

"Crikey", said Douglas "I'm soaked again - wot'll we do"
William, ever the inventive one suggested a game out in the open skimming objects across the frozen pond and that would soon dry them off. "We'll get warm doing that and the water will 'vaprate. We did that in science so it can be a sort of 'speriment, my Dad is always saying we shud be back n' skool cos of the learning we are missing. It'll show 'em we needn't be in skool to lurn stuff!"

A happy half hour passed until the frozen pond was littered with an impressive range of objects that had been recovered from the layer of snow at the edge of the pond. Sticks, stones, fir cones and a couple of bottles had all been slid across the ice much to the outlaws amusement. The thick ice had resisted the barrage of objects and the outlaws had just started debating whether they should look further afield for a fresh supply of missiles or were they prepared to walk across the ice and collect the objects for reuse.

Douglas was the most emphatic -

"If that ice breaks we'll be even wetter than we are already -that's if you don't drown 'an if I don't drown my Mum'll kill me if I get home this wet. An' another thing my clothes are wetter now than before so i'm not sure your right about this 'vaporatin."

Warming to his argument, if not his wet clothes he continued - "I don't think your right about the ice easily supporting us - I think you've proved your knowledge of science is flimsy" pausing dramatically he added "Like the ice! I'm gonna look for more stuff to skim" and he squelched off in his wet socks and wellies.

The three remaining outlaws spent the next few minutes speculating on the part of the pond where the ice looked thickest and were now arguing who was the lightest and in the unlikely event of one of them falling in which of them would be strongest to haul the other one out. The inconclusive but noisy debate was cut short by Douglas who after having unearthed several small sticks was now wrestling with another one pointing out of a bank of snow nearby.

"Come here - I've got something interesting"
There was something in his voice for the others to abandon their argument, which wasn't making much progress, and to walk over to where he was standing.
Douglas was standing next to a bank of snow staring down at a long pointed curved object, a sort of quill, pointing out of the snow with some round speckled object to the side.
"I think it's a bird said Douglas. It's cold."
"Course it's cold - it's covered in snow, get it out" said Ginger.
"It's dead" said Henry who tended towards the morbid.
"It's probably 'ibernating" said William emphatically anxious to regain some respect for his scientific expertise which stood in severe danger of being discredited by recent events.
Gently and tentatively the snow was scraped away from the large speckled bird to reveal a long curved beak and long spindly legs. It was still immobile.
There was now the dilemma as to what to do with this exciting new discovery. Henry produced a plastic bag from his coat pocket. This was hardly surprising as much to the exasperation of their parents the pockets of the outlaws were long term stores of miscellaneous objects. Veritable miniature tool-sheds
containing string, penknives, elastic as well as maturing forgotten biscuit fragments, sweets and fruit, bus tickets, as well as the occasional precious hauls of low value coins.
The silent and solid form of the bird was carefully scooped into the carrier bag with only the beak protruding out of the top. The Outlaws now engaged in a passionate argument over their next course of action. On the one side was Henry and Douglas who were advocates of the hibernation theory and strongly supported a visit to the local vet for an emergency revival. This was equally strongly opposed by William and Ginger who favoured a visit to the local museum in town which they remembered visiting on a recent school trip.
"They've got all sorts of rare animals, n' fish, n' birds in there but they've not got one of these - I bet it's really rare, could be the last survivor, maybe people already think it's 'xtinct -

probably a reward might be paid or at least a notice on display with us as 'splorers wot discovered it!"
This was quite a persuasive argument but the decision was finally sealed by Ginger who clinched it with the statement - "Well your parents said you can't ever go the vets again after wot Jumble did to that rabbit there…"
William cut this unpleasant memory short by picking up the carrier and loudly stating -"Let's go to the museum now. It's quite a walk but it'll be worth it."
The argument forgotten all the four seemed relieved that a course of action was agreed and they set off throughout the snow towards the coast road that led to the museum a mile away. They chatted animatedly and quite forgot how wet they were and cheerily disregarded the tellings off awaiting them at home. All of this would be eclipsed by the news of the discovery. "Should think that may want to call up the radio and TV people to show off the new exhibit - s'not often they would be able to exhibit an extinct bird." The significance of the discovery was growing rapidly in William's mind and his natural exuberance was infectious to the others. That is except for Henry who was getting quieter as they neared the large pillared building that was the museum. He stopped them several yards away and said confidently - "there's not lights on. I think they've shut jus' like the school. The heatings probably off, 'an they'll have removed all the precious stuff cos of burst pipes an stuff damaging things. We'd better come back - we can put the bird in my fridge I don't 'spose my Mum will mind - there's already some joint left from Sunday - it'll probably keep for ages. Then you can come back later in the week - when the lights are on, or the snow's gone."
His confident plan of action almost convinced the others but William had a flash of suspicion about this.
"I remember now, you got into trouble on the school trip - yes, you said one of the stuffed animals was imprisoned in the glass case and was alive, you swore its eyes moved."
Douglas joined in -"Yes, 'an when sir took no notice and told you not to be so stupid you hammered on the glass so hard - the fox didn't move but the magpie on the branch above came off it's perch and its head fell off." The head museum

keeper said you should never be let in there again and called you an hooligan or something."
Henry stood his ground and said anyway he wasn't coming in and would wait for them by the steps.
By this time William had taken matters in hand and after pressing the round brass door bell was now using the large brass door knocker with his usual level of enthusiasm. It achieved a fairly quick result as lights could be seen coming on and the large panelled door creaked open and from behind it came a rather annoyed man in a dark uniform.
"What do you want ?" he asked loudly and angrily.
"We are closed for the duration."
At the same time he suspiciously regarded what he could see of Henry who was trying to hide behind Ginger, unsuccessfully as Ginger was some inches shorter than he was.
"Don't I know that one- why do I think that?"
The Outlaws resisted reminding him instead William thrust the carrier bag towards him and exclaimed with some authority "We've discovered a rare bird, it might be dead - or 'ibernatin " anxious to hedge his bets in case the bird revived, " But anyway, it's likely to be an extinct one and we are the discoverers. So we'll give you our names for the plaque and stuff."
The man peered into the bag and looked back at them.
"What do you expect me to do this." He thrust the bag to a startled and exceedingly disappointed William who took hold of it and was about to eloquently argue their case when the man, now getting red in the face shouted "Now clear off the lot of you ... and you," he said to Henry "you are banned for life!"
It was a disconsolate band that trudged the two miles home through the snow. Henry had withdrawn his offer of housing the prize exhibit in his fridge having got cold feet on the idea to add to the cold feet in his wellingtons. William had tired of carrying the bag and had passed it to Ginger who was sniffing the bag and announce he didn't think it was going to revive and that he thought it was starting to smell a bit. Reluctantly they dumped the prize in the next roadside bin they came to.

William conclude the adventure by somewhat indignantly stating -"I dunno how museums get anything to exhibit if that's how they treat people - I think he didn't want to be shown up by not knowing about rare or 'extinct creatures." This was met with universal grunts and nods of agreement by the others who were now anticipating the reaction to the welcome they would be receiving at home in their damp and dejected state. The discovery of the dead curlew, for that was what it was, was never mentioned to their parents and the episode was chalked up as yet another example of the unreasonable nature of the adult world.

Both these episodes are substantially true with the names change and dialogue adapted. What is consistent is the childhood sense of outrage in both circumstances. If anyone is not familiar with the William Brown stories and wants to recapture the absurdity of the adult world when viewed with childhood sensibilities then I heartily recommend the books as an antidote to the abundance of misery literature currently being published.

Dad's first car

Car ownership was far from universal in Britain in the years of my early childhood. I remember my grand father, my Mum's Dad, had a car but can't recall travelling in it only seeing it parked outside their house and them driving it to see us. More significantly I remember my father acquiring our first car when I was around six or seven.It's not strictly true that Dad was the first car owner in the house because I have photo of me as a five year old wedged in a pedal car that looked too small for me and I think it was soon passed

on to my brother but not before I had enjoyed the ownership all too briefly including repainting it, silver I believe. Probably using the same aluminium paint from the more disastrous knight's armour incident.The second photo looks like I have driven down the garden for an impromptu Teddy Bear's picnic. The car was an upgrade from my metal horse on wheels christened 'Blackie' although photos suggest it was black and white - isn't that piebald? Still who wants to own a

horse called Baldie or Pie come to that. At the same time my younger brother owned a small wooden horse and cart that he had christened 'Horse-collar !'
Yes, it was mystery to us too - I am sure he was pleased to graduate to the enhanced street cred of the pedal car.
My first memory of my Dad's car is travelling in the back while my father was having driving lessons given by my uncle, his elder brother. Dad had learned to drive in the army although this was mostly in the desert according to him and had apparently not extended to gaining any sort of licence. The lessons were to prepare for the test and to get used to traffic and road signs and other skills not required for desert driving.They seemed to consist of drives in the summer evenings in country lanes from our house. The journeys were punctuated by unplanned roadside stops where Dad and my uncle would open the bonnet and peer inside, prod and tap things and usually emerge with oily hands that had to be wiped on a rag after which the car would or would not restart after being subjected to some muttered swearing mostly by my Dad as my Uncle Trevor was a chapel preacher and probably more temperate in his language. I assumed such pit stops were all part of car ownership and already learned that 'cleaning the plugs' was a more regular occurrence than buying petrol.
The car was kept on hard standing at the end of our garden and accessed by a narrow lane between the back of the houses in our road and the wall of the cemetery next door. The car was what I believed is known as a 'sit up and beg' Ford Anglia. The sort that in recent years I have occasionally seen customised as an American style hot rod. A little research has suggested it was probably produced in the late 1940's. I recall it being difficult to start and remember one episode when my father was in the front of the car turning a starter handle and had enlisted my Mum to sit in the car pressing the accelerator. I was sitting in the front seat with her, and my father, between winding the handle and groaning and probably swearing under his breath, was instructing her to "keep pulling the choke out!"
This she did with what proved to be rather too much enthusiasm as I saw several feet of cable emerge through

the dash as she pulled the choke knob completely out. A request from him of whether she was definitely 'pulling out the choke?' was met with her dangling the choke knob and several feet of attached cable out of the car window. His reaction was not one of pleasure. We were at home outside the house and I think I was sent back in the house 'to play.' The acquisition of a family car meant not only that our travel horizons could be extended beyond the range of local bus routes but also the tedium of waiting at bus stops could be a thing of the past at least when my Dad wasn't at work. Family days out now included trips to Pembrokeshire and the countryside of Carmarthenshire as well as welcome trips to the funfairs of Porthcawl and Barry Island. The waterfalls of the South Wales valleys were also popular picnic spots and one thing I remember was buying small triangular car stickers recording places visited such as Caerphilly Castle and then putting these in the car window as a sort of token show of our sophistication and extent of our travel. The car allowed us later to have holidays further afield and to visit relatives around the country.

Some families seem to acquire a brand loyalty to a make of car, rather like the political allegiances in families in the US. "Yes the Edwards family are Democrats, always have been - grandad Edward Edwards, Ed Edwards Jnr, and lill' Eddie." Similar loyalties with families having a long succession of Fords or Rovers - "we don't hold with these new fangled Japanese cars." My father had no brand loyalty that I could remember. The sequence of cars that I can recall, and I've probably missed some included, in approximate chronological order, the following automotive gems:-

The first one was a black Ford Anglia from I believe the late 1940's.

There was a brief ownership of some kind of grey convertible 4 seater from Standard that I remember had an enamel union jack flag as part of its bonnet badge. Apparently it also had cable operated brakes that failed on a steep hill in Swansea and almost killed my Dad when it mounted the pavement and came to a halt by hitting a tree! He never owned a Triumph (that Standard combined with) and I can't

say I blame him. He must have looked at my Triumph Herald with some cynicism.
This was followed by an Austin A30 in grey.
A new Ford Popular in canary yellow.
I am unsure of the exact order here but there were
a Morris Traveller with the wooden 'shooting brake' adornments.
A more more modern Ford Popular that was cozy shaped and had some bizarre method of driving the windscreen wipers from the pressure in the manifold (?) so that the faster you would drive, the slower the wipers speed would be. Even as a child I could recognise this as a design fault.

This was followed by a better 1960's Ford Anglia with the reverse sloping back window in two tone grey and yellow I think.
A Mini that was the Austin model.
A Hillman Minx which had a front bench seat and seemed quite a luxurious car.
The last car of my childhood was a Hillman Imp that was the first car of his that I drove once I had passed my driving test.
After that there was a BMC 1100 and after I left home he revived his Ford ownership with a Ford Cortina estate and rather rakish and pseudo American Ford Corsair that had tail fins.
His later years were spent in more reliable Volkswagens, a VW beetle and some VW Polos.
Looking at the list maybe he was a Ford man at heart. He didn't ever own a French car, maybe it was the memory of being on the beach at Dunkirk and I can recall him casting disparaging remarks about my uncle's Renault Dauphine saying it looked a bit like a boat and it was difficult to tell which end was the front!
I have only owned two Fords, both company cars and sadly my Dad didn't live to see my VW camper van but I think he would have approved.
My own car ownership is recorded in my book also published on Amazon - "Tracks of my Tyres."

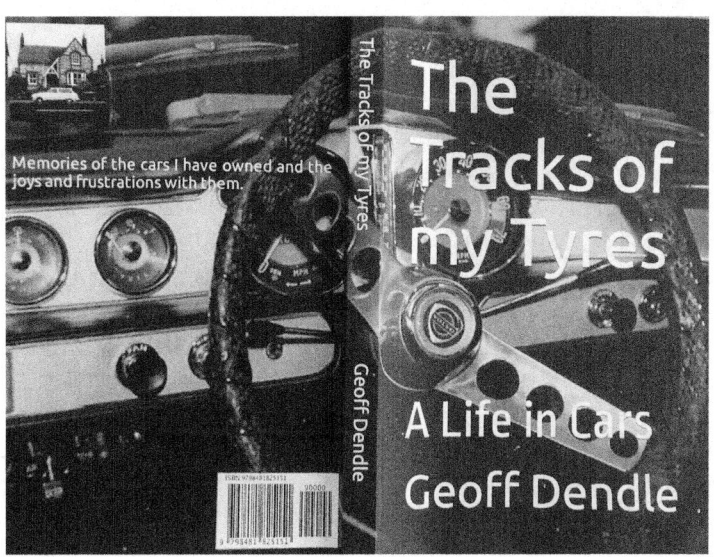

The Tracks of my Tyres

Memories of the cars I have owned and the joys and frustrations with them.

A Life in Cars
Geoff Dendle

Pets

The first pet that was truly mine was a hamster.
Before this there had been a short interlude when my brother and me had been the proud owners of two black and white rabbits. They were called bizarrely Jimmy and Nibbles and ownership was disputed as they seemed identical and shared a hutch made I recall by my Dad. They had arrived in the house following a visit one summer to an uncle of my Mum's in Wiltshire.
We must have been returning from a holiday either in Gloucester with my Mum's twin brother who was stationed in the airforce there or from another aunt in Essex. I don't remember which but summer holidays in my early childhood were invariably spent with relatives who would make return visits to us to enjoy the Welsh beaches
Uncle Jim we discovered was a champion owner and breeder of rabbits and the walls of his garden were lined with hutches containing many of them. At the time I didn't realise that they were mostly being raised to eat and my parents wisely protected me from the shock of this reality. I do remember commenting at some stage that uncle Jim must really like Rabbits and my Dad's knowing reply - "Oh yes, he really likes rabbit!" the subtly of this being lost on my eight year's vocabulary. We had been shown two small black and white rabbits described as Dutch in origin and asked if we would like them - then looking at my Dad he added "as pets- if you like."
Somehow they were conveyed home, probably in cardboard box in the family Ford Anglia. Once at home, in short order, my father had constructed a wooden hutch for them to live in. We would supply them with vegetables and maybe there was rabbit food as well as there was a pet food shop in the next village. I recollect that everything was fine until out of kindness it was suggested that they would enjoy the freedom of running around the garden and chewing some fresh dandelions and clover. All went well until the family cat came in the garden and fearing some rabbit massacre I called my Mum who arrived in time to see the two small rabbits "ganging up" on the cat and chasing it up the cherry

tree in the middle of the lawn. Everyone was amused, apart from the cat who stayed up there until the rabbits were put back in their hutch. Their rabbit rampage was not complete - they had started biting off the flower heads in the garden borders and were recaptured by me and put away before the damage was too noticeably. Unfortunately, as my Mum was unaware of this and knowing that they seemed to be able to take care of themselves, as for as the cat was concerned, Mum had allowed them free range in the garden while I was at school. The damage was extensive, hardly a flower head was intact apart from the climbing roses. That evening there

was a family discussion and their fate was sealed. The cat was avoiding going out, the garden had no flowers and unbeknown to me Jimmy and Nibbles may have already lived longer than if they had stayed with Uncle Jimmy, their namesake. Rescue was at hand though as one of my classmates was an ambitious small animal breeder and already had mice, rats, rabbits and guinea pigs in cages in a summer house in his garden.

Children being the kind souls they are he had already acquired the prefix "pregnant' to his surname although it was acknowledged that he had a useful additional revenue stream to his pocket money, I later heard he qualified as an accountant !

"You must ask David if he would like them" said my Mum with my Dad adding "Tell him they come with the cage" - anxious to restore family tranquility and no doubt thinking an empty cage in the garden might lead to other unwelcome acquisitions.

So it temporally ended my first period of pet ownership. There was also the family cat but I did not regard it as belonging to me and beyond him being ginger and rather unimaginably called Sandy I don't recall having much of a relationship. There appears not to be any photos of him being dressed up or wearing face paint of the kind popularised today on social media. I can only conclude he was either too fierce or too aloof in a cat type way to not engage with children.

While I think of it, for my parents to think it safe for a hamster to be introduced into the family, he was probably one of those cats that lived to just eat and sleep. Whatever, I was provided with Hammy the hamster on I think my tenth birthday, probably after a period of extensive lobbying on my behalf. He was also named rather unimaginatively after the TV hamster of the same name in the series "Tales of the Riverbank." Today, having watched some original footage of the programme I realise what a dangerous life he must have led although he lived almost the full hamster lifespan of eighteen months to two years having the good grace to pass away while I was also away at scout camp.

The series showed various adventures of the hamster and his friend Roddy, a white rat, with voices of the animals provided by Johnnie Morris. Some of their exploits were recreated by my younger brother and myself with the hamster's apparent enthusiastic cooperation although I suspect he was just pleased to be let out of his cage and possibly over anxious to be up at what was to him the middle of the night.

The re-enacted exploits included sailing him on our small garden pond; sending him around the lawn in a clockwork car that he constantly escaped from to eat clover and dandelion leaves, one of his favourite delicacies along with peas. The hamster was spared any involvement in the more ambitious storylines in the TV series but I am confident that if we had access to a flying model aircraft or a balloon then his life may have been more adventurous not to mention perilous. I am just thinking that he was fortunate that his lifespan did not overlap with the ownership of Jack's rocket as the reaction to requesting the return of the rocket and 'hamsternaut' from a neighbouring garden is hard to imagine. I am sure the RSPCA would be called.

The hamster's enthusiasm for leftover vegetables led to my younger brother and me vying as to who could leave the most vegetables on our plates -'for Hammy as he gets bored with hamster food!'

My Dad would darkly mutter that he wouldn't fit in the cage if he ate all that. The hamster was never his favourite after the overcoat disaster. I don't really recall what happened about the overcoat repair or whether Hammy carried on with overnighting in the cupboard, presumably with anything else a safe distance from the bars.

That is one thing the pet shop had not mentioned - hamsters are nocturnal and with poor eyesight prefer to be up and about in the dark so his initial home in my bedroom was less than ideal because at night his activities were not designed to allow anyone in the same room a good nights sleep. His repertoire of noisy activities were all amplified by the metal cage he lived in and included noisily gnawing anything he fancied in the cage including the metal bars and according to the 'Know your Hamster' book we had the gnawing was necessary to keep his teeth down which constantly grew unless checked.

The book ambitiously suggested that home care of overgrown hamsters teeth could be dealt with by using nail scissors to avoid a visit to the vets. Even at my tender age I knew this to be mad advice and that was without asking the hamster for his opinion about it!

 The book also advised placing pieces of clean wood and even wooden cotton reels in is cage for this purpose. The latter were not a great success as his attempts to gnaw the edge of them seemed to make them noisily ricochet around the cage with him hanging on. The other noise generator was his exercise wheel which he would noisily use for hours on end and no amount of lubrication seemed able to quieten it going from mild squeaking to amplified grinding noise. A solution was found with unexpected results. Downstairs off the living room was a cupboard under the stairs so it was suggested that his cage was kept on the sideboard and at our bedtime after he had been up and 'playing' for our enjoyment for a couple of hours our bedtime he would see him transferred to the dark cupboard where behind a closed door he could enjoy his nocturnal activities with minimum disruption to the rest of the household. I am guessing that this arrangement worked satisfactorily for a period of time but the arrangements were to come to an abrupt end when one morning the 'getting ready' for work and school activities were rudely interrupted by a loud shout of "Bloody Hell" - my Dad's favourite curse. Arriving in the living room we all found my father with the cupboard door open, standing in his best winter tweed overcoat and poking his whole hand out through a large round hole in the material.

The culprit was discovered sleeping in his newly lined woollen bed after what must have been a hard nights chewing through the bars of his cage to harvest his new, improved bedding from my Dads overcoat hanging on the back of the cupboard door and presumably resting temptingly up against the bars of the cage. My Mum's suggestion that she may be able to darn it and perhaps it wouldn't show did not seem to help matters. Remembering the abrupt end to our short period as rabbit owners we were relieved returning from school that day to find that Hammy was still a member of the family and he went on to live the full hamster lifespan of almost two years. As I said earlier he had the good grace to expire while I was away at Cub camp and continued to provide entertainment even from beyond the grave, this time to a busload of people! My Mum was left with instructions about his food, cleaning, emptying his jam jar (yes hamsters can be trained to use their own toilet, after all he had already proved to my Dad he could make his own bed!) Also, that on no account was my younger brother to handle him - this was probably unnecessary advice as my brother showed an understandable reluctance to do so having had his fingers nipped by him on several occasions.

I was not fully appraised of events, no doubt to limit the trauma, but to summarise it appears that some time during my absence the hamster was similarly not seen 'out an about' so as to speak in his cage so after a day our two my Mum found him curled up motionless in his bed and gentle prodding didn't rouse him. Placing him in a small cardboard box my Mum and brother took him on the bus to the vet, not for a post mortem but to establish that he wasn't hibernating. Swansea buses of that time could be akin to a mobile social event and it wasn't long before the passengers were involved in a game of "what's in the box?" that Mum had been carrying so carefully. A game which developed into a game of "Dead or not Dead?" as the box was passed around the bus. I am unable to tell you whether the passengers included any with relevant medical or veterinary expertise but this was later provided by the vet. Short of banging the small rodent on the desk he more or less re-enacted the Monty Python dead parrot sketch yet to be inflicted on the public. He also relayed the pearl of wisdom that hibernation is rather rare in July, even in Wales. So ended my first foray into livestock management.

I recall now that there was an earlier pet in the household, one that required little attention and seemed to pretty much cater for himself. One summer we had a visit from a cousin of my Mum's and her husband who called to see us while staying nearby in Gower. They had driven down from London in an open car, an MG roadster or something similar and whilst stopped at some roadworks had looked down to see a 'stone' moving in the gutter. It was a
Tortoise so they rescued it and would we like it - there was only one answer - Of course. So Torty (I know - no imagination!) the tortoise came to live with us. Once the cat had got over it's initial curiosity the reptile was left to wander about in the garden and with occasion feedings of lettuce and carrots it was pretty low maintenance. The only drama I remember was occasionally finding him upside down on his back after overambitious mountaineering attempt in the rockery and needing to right him.
Our first family dog was I think acquired accidentally in the sense that he was bought as a puppy from the pet shop Swansea market.

When I think of the processes gone through in later life for

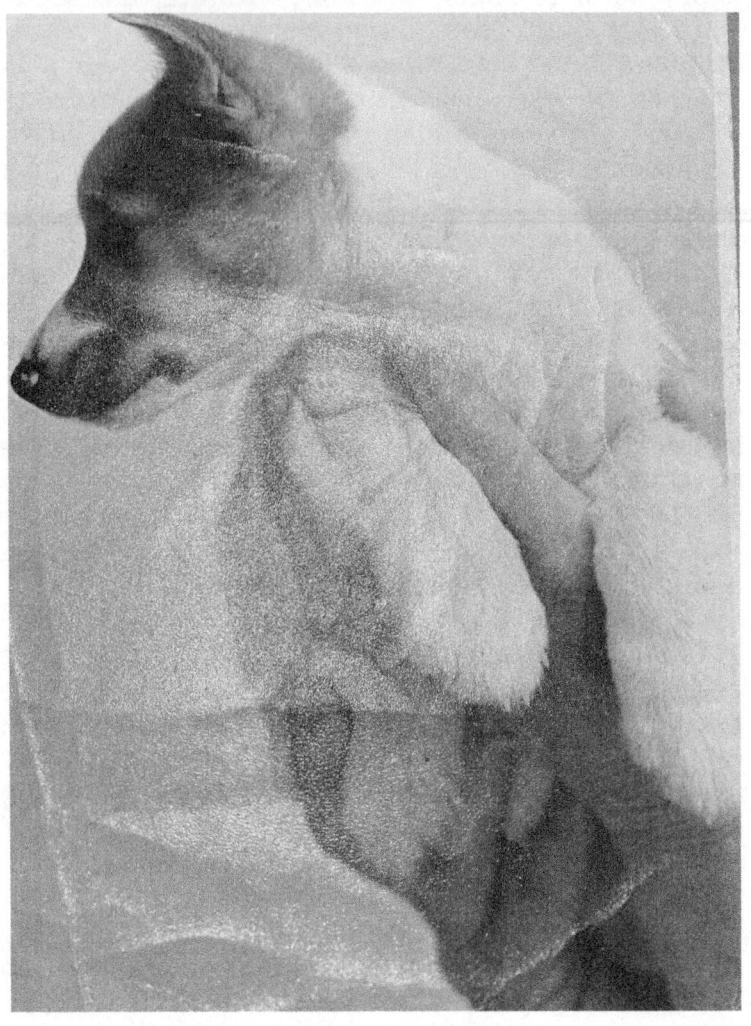

acquiring any of the five dogs that I have owned as an adult the comparison is rather stark.

Two of our dogs came as pedigrees from breeders where we met the owners and the dog's mother and provided details of where we lived and the space available at the home. These were both Irish Wolfhounds and given their massive size such details are not trivial. The other dogs were rescue dogs and in those cases we were interviewed at home and the potential environment was inspected.

The market pet stall had rabbits, kittens, guinea pigs and small chicks in cages and fish in tanks and it was always a destination when visiting town and the market with my parents. I am sure we pestered for pets on other occasions but for some reason this day we were successful. I was later reminded by Mum that he cost two pounds and ten shillings. Photos from the time show him as a small puppy able to be held up in two adult hands. He was white with a brown head and a brown patch on one side and described as a 'cross-bred' corgi fox terrier. He certainly had a corgi's head but had longer legs once fully grown and I believe he was my early birthday present so I claimed him as my dog and was in charge of feeding him and allowed to take him out for walks and sometimes he slept on my bed. I loved him to bits! The corgi part of him had something of a character and this was a mixed blessing. He took against some of my and my brother's friends when visiting and could be territorial. This trait proved beneficial as I was allowed freer range to go out to local parks and woods on the theory that I was offered protection by this feisty fur ball. Before I went to secondary school there was a brief period that we owned a family caravan and this was another opportunity to roam the sand dunes and the north Gower beach and Llanmadoc with our small band of boys under the 'protection' of my fierce and loyal dog. This probably gave us a taste for later adventures with the scouts when we considered ourselves too grown up to need guard dogs.

The photos here appear to show Patch as a puppy being introduced to a very dubious cat, Sandy with the second photo some time later with the cat still harbouring a grudge.

Buses

Unfortunately the 'guess the mortality of the hamster' episode was not my Mum's most embarrassing bus journey. I was to provide two of these some years earlier.
I would contend, whilst sounding like an old fogey, that children in the 1950's needed far more patience than subsequent generations. The interminable afternoons spent at relatives or friends of your parents house without the distraction of a smart phone or an iPad. "Didn't you bring a book or your comic to read? Why don't you play with the cat (not to be recommended as cats in houses visited for afternoon tea were always of a violent disposition) and the subsequent and inevitable minor wound was usually met with an unsympathetic reaction of "you must have been teasing it - it's normally so friendly. Why don't you look out the window for a while."
This exercise of patience had to also applied to the dreaded 'waiting for the bus.' Although bus timetables were published and occasionally were displayed on some bus stops it was rare for family outings concluding at the bus stop to neatly coincide with a short wait for the bus to take us home. There were waits that seemed to take hours although we were fortunate that there were two routes home to Tycoch, one on the number 75, this one took a route through another suburb of Sketty and usually took longer but was relatively frequent. The other was a number 33 that took a more direct route up the steep hill to Glanmor. Both those buses terminated in Tycoch square. That route was also served by a number 23 that followed the route for over three quarters of the way before veering off to foreign parts such as Fforestfach, a place like many in Wales that seemed oversupplied with 'f's.' This particular day a 23 bus came along first and my mother either out of desperation of entertaining a 4 year old and a toddler in a push chair elected to catch the 23 and bought us tickets for the Broadway stop. All was well until at that stop my mother alighted first with my toddler brother and the push chair and was either expecting the conductor (remember them?) to help me down to her from the open rear platform or was

going to lift me down after she had secured my brother in the pushchair. For whatever reason, this did not occur, instead the conductor who may have not noticed me still standing on the platform pressed the bell and the bus drove away and I saw my mother and brother on the pavement getting further away. Apparently, my screams were sufficient to be heard over the noise of the engine and either the driver or the conductor stopped the bus and my potential abduction was averted. Apparently, according to my mother I was not a confident bus passenger for a while and the number 23 bus was avoided thereafter.

 As if this episode of bus drama wasn't embarrassing enough I had previously exceeded it at a younger age when travelling on the bus alone with my my Mum prior to the arrival of my younger brother. I don't know the age but under two I suspect as I had been experimenting with talking and according to my Mum who regularly recalled this tale throughout my life had recently mastered a new word to add to MMaa and DDaa. The extension to this repertoire had been courtesy of the family cat who I had christened Aaannnggg probably because of the noise he would make when I could corner him "to play with."
Sitting down on the bus with me sitting on my Mum's lap it seems my attention was attracted to the fur collar of the lady who had got onto the bus a little while into our journey and was quietly sitting on the seat in front of us. Before I could be stopped I leant forward and started stroking the fur collar while delightedly and proudly repeating my new word at the top of my voice - "aaanngg! aaanngg! AAANNGG!"
Pulling me and my hand out of reach my mother quickly apologised to the lady but this didn't stop my repeated cries of " AAANNGG! AAANNGG! AAANNGG!" The lady turned round looking concerned so my mother thinking quickly explained to her that this was my new word for something that I liked. I was relatively new to the world of the spoken word and by this stage I was engaged in some elaborate imitation of a cat with mimed claws and pointed ear mimes. Apparently one of my earliest theatrical performances.
Needless to say we left the bus at the next stop - I don't

know if it was our intended one but I did notice that my Mum would nervously regard fellow passengers on buses for a while, at least until I could differentiate between living animals and fur coats.

I am pretty sure that on occasions my Mum would walk us into town or at least to the Uplands where my grandmother lived. It was mostly downhill and I guess there was the bribery of a walk downhill and the bus ride uphill on the way home. Unless of course my Mum was still suffering bouts of 'bus embarrassment' thanks to the earlier episode. The walk was enlivened by simple entertainment - spot the animals - this opportunity was two fold. Firstly looking for lizards that in the warm weather could be seen basking on the wall top near Glanmor school. Quite why they were so common there I can't say as I don't remember seeing lizards so regularly in one place in this country. More popular to me was looking for animal and other patterns in the crazy paving wall that extended along this road for several hundred yards.I am grateful to the imaginative stonemason who had taken the time some years previously to create the outlines of a dozen or more animals and sailing boats in the stonework of the wall next to the pavement. I am sure, until the novelty wore off, it was used by Mum to bribe us on the walk.

Fires and dramatic events

It's perhaps not surprising that it's easier to remember the details of the more dramatic events in the past than the routinely mundane and this seems true of childhood. It's difficult to remember details of the numerous walks to school, or individual lessons and in the same way one family meal was much like another and they merge together in the memory. So it takes a small piece of drama to bring back to mind sitting around the kitchen table one day my Mum, Dad, my brother and myself. Of course I can't remember what the meal was but it must have been hot and savoury. Maybe it was fish and chips but a small moment of minor drama etched it on my memory. The range of sauces and condiments in those days was very limited to ordinary families in comparison with the huge range available today, I can only remember, salad cream, tomato sauce and brown sauce which I liked and Branston pickle and English mustard which I didn't. My Dad was particularly partial to tomato sauce or ketchup. I remember that it was sometimes sluggish to come out of the bottle and could be coaxed by a drop of vinegar and a vigorous shaking the bottle up and down, usually executed by my Dad. Whether the sauce had been diluted that day and the cap not tightly screwed on or whether it had been previously returned to the larder in a 'loosened' state and lurked there for some days like an unexploded bomb - who knows? My Dad vigorously shook the bottle and a thick stream of the red sauce flew out and hit the ceiling with some force with splattering falling back on us, the table cloth and the floor - the bottle was virtually empty. We were both sent off to wash and change while I expect some rather heated post mortem on events took place in the kitchen now resembling a scene from a Hammer horror film.
I am unsure of the sequence of events but he kitchen ceiling was the scene of another 'red' incident. The ceiling was equipped with a range of pipes probably to serve the range and the sink taps I don't know but I do remember returning from school one afternoon for my Mum to proudly show off her painting inspiration that she had worked on that day.

She had painted all of the pipes bright red! On reflection had she been inspired by the ketchup disaster or was she predicting it or was she providing inspiration to Richard Rogers and Renzo Piano for the Pompidou centre in Paris and yet to be built?
The conclusion was provided by my Dad , "It's like being on board ship again - it looks like a boiler room!" Clearly he was reluctant to be reminded of the few years spent in the merchant navy as a teenager in the late 1930's. The weekend saw my Dad up a ladder repainting the pipes white - I believe it took several coats!

Fire was a constant source of danger in the 1950's home. It was hardly surprising for although the population had largely moved on from domestic gas lighting and was yet to be seduced by such frippery as smelly meditation candles there were other convenient sources of danger. Firstly, the majority of adults smoked. Apart from the cigarettes and pipes themselves there were the hazards of the accompanying paraphernalia - the smouldering ashtrays in unattended rooms, abundant supplies of matches or table lighters to tempt curious children. There was the similar and arguably more hazardous pipe smokers which apart from the dreadful smell were often setting light to clothing after putting a hot pipe away in a jacket or cardigan pocket. Whoever thought it safe to drive around in a petrol fuelled metal box filled with plastic covered foam furniture and nylon carpets while having what amounts to a small personal brazier several inches from their face whilst keeping the fire stoked by puffing air through it. Madness !!
Years later as an adult I participated in the evacuation of a five storey office building on Hove seafront along with five hundred others and watched as the fire brigade turned up to attend to a fire in an office waste paper bin caused by the emptying of a pipe into it before the person left the room. At the time the culprit headed up the company's 'think tank' - certainly made me think!
So apart from the dangers of smoking we had the hazards provided by coal fires, gas stoves lit with matches or paper tapers, portable paraffin heaters as well as the general

unreliability of old electrical appliances with fraying fabric leads in houses with no circuit breaker safety systems - it's a wonder we're still here.
Chimney fires seemed to be a not uncommon occurrence in the roads around us. You would see dense black smoke coming out of the chimney and then the fire brigade would arrive - very exciting for small children. We managed to have one in our house and by the time a neighbour knocked on the door we knew something was wrong as there was a noise like a jet engine coming down the chimney. The fires were caused when sparks or flames from the fireplace were able to set alight any deposits of soot that had collected on ledges in the house chimney itself. A good way to start one, so we discovered to our cost, was to place a 'damper' in our case a metal plate with a handle that covered the fireplace opening but allowed air to be drawn from below where the ash tray was to oxygenate a reluctant fire. We had, I think recently acquired one to replace my Dad's previous more risky method of placing a sheet of newspaper over the opening to 'draw the fire.' The newspaper was either removed when the fire roared and the coals caught with flames being seen behind the paper or more frequently (and dangerously) when the newspaper caught fire and either was poked back into the fire or stamped on in the hearth by my Dad whilst shouting '"Bloody Hell!" depending on the quality of footwear, shoes were fine - slippers or socks less so.

I believe the damper had been left in place by my Dad and he was only alerted to the problem when we called him to say there was a noise up the chimney.
I think we were sent out in the back garden on this occasion which had the advantage of seeing the smoke coming out of the chimney but meant we'd miss the fire brigade if they came as they would come up the road in front of the house. I don't recall them coming so I think that disaster was averted by the fire going out once the damper was removed or he had thrown water in the fireplace and the resulting steam had ended things.
In fact, I don't recall the fire brigade ever coming to our house. This may be due to the lack of a phone in our house

or any immediate neighbours so a 999 would have to be made from a public phone box near the shops on the Square or by asking one of the shops to use theirs. There were other occasions when they may have needed to attend. I recall a fire on a clothes horse where clothes had been left in front of the fire - I guess the stamping feet method was deployed but I remember the smell of burnt wool lingering for some days.

There were also the TV and Radio fires. I don't know whether it was the unreliability of old, valve operated appliances or the gathering of dust inside them but I recall two episodes where flames appeared from the back of the TV and on another occasion the radio.
The radio was doused in water by my Dad which certainly put out the fire and I guess ruined the set beyond economic repair. I think it was too big and heavy to run out through the kitchen and into the back garden with it though this was the method deployed by my Dad for the TV fire. I still have a vision in my mind of us screaming while my Dad picked the television off its table and ran out of the room with flames still emerging from the back of the set. He only paused to duck as the plug whizzed past his head as he hadn't unplugged it from the mains!
Again the smell lingered a while at home, an acid, dry electrical smell. I suppose replacing either of these appliances was an expense that we could have done without. I said earlier that I don't think the fire brigade ever came to our house and while that is true our family did not entirely escape from using their expertise. Sadly, I didn't witness the event first hand but coming home from infants school one afternoon I found my younger and pre school brother sitting quietly and looking sorry for himself with a rather red face and particularly red ears. Asking my Mum what had happened and trying to stop herself from laughing she explained that as I would probably hear the story in school the next day she would tell me. The fire brigade had attended the school that afternoon unbeknown to me but the incident had been outside the school - on the pavement.

Returning home past the school that afternoon with our Mum my brother had taken it upon himself to thrust his head through the school railings. Gentle coaxing followed by more vigorous persuasion, judging by the colour of his ears, had proved unsuccessful and together with his crying had resulted in an emergency call to the fire brigade. Thankfully, they arrived promptly and using some mechanical means bent the cast iron railings enough free him. I am not sure whether I was more sorry to have missed the drama or whether it was tempered by my gratitude to the head teacher for preserving the family's anonymity during his speech on the inherent dangers of railings and heads. It's a pity that my brother wasn't present for the lecture as several weeks later we had to have our gas cooker temporarily disconnected to free my brothers head from behind it. I was present to witness this but I would have rather seen the fire engine!

Holidays

For the average family in the 1950's holidays were less ambitious than today. The era of package holidays, low cost flights and city breaks at all times of the year was some way off. When I compare the holidays then, one week in the summer, with our own travels in recent years it's of a completely different order. That's not to say my parents hadn't travelled already. My Mums WAAF service in the war hadn't included any bombing missions over Germany although after peace was declared she did fly over Belgium and Germany one day in an RAF plane to see the damage which was pretty sobering. More memorable to her was living in Jamaica for several years prior to grammar school back here in the 1930's. We have photos of her and her brothers sitting with their parents on a veranda shaded by palm trees and riding horses on sandy beaches. She would talk fondly of picking pineapples and avocados in the garden as well as eating sugar cane - all sounding very exotic in 1950's post rationing Britain.
My grandfather was a Regimental Sergeant Major in the Royal engineers and claimed to be in Jamaica building infrastructure which sounds plausible. For part of the war the family lived in Coventry which was badly bombed and at that time he was an air raid warden so must have seen many opportunities for infrastructure repair!
My own father had travelled extensively. Firstly in his teens in the merchant navy on the SS Tewkesbury and from what I remember the sailings of this cargo ship included visits to ports in South America, South Africa and the USA and Caribbean. His wartime travels included being evacuated from the beach at Dunkirk, service in the army in North Africa, Egypt, Italy and Palestine. I am not sure any of it could be described as a holiday although he described Spike Milligan's humorous wartime memoirs as the most accurate portrayal that he had read.
Our own family holidays were a lot nearer home.
They often consisted of a car journey to stay with relatives, usually my uncle Doug and his family who lived between Gloucester and Cheltenham and was my brother's twin and

in the RAF. It was also home to my cousins Helen and Amanda. The first holiday that I have only a vague memory of was to go by coach to Aberystwyth for us all to stay with my Auntie Minnie my Dad's aunt. This must have been before we had the family car and I remember that it was the longest bus journey of my life at that time - up to three hours with stops. My brother was still in a push chair so I would have been four or five. I can't recall much about the holiday other than Aunt Minnie's house was by a bridge next to the river and because of this I couldn't go outside unsupervised. Also the beach was disappointedly stony with

us being used to the beautiful sandy beaches at home in Swansea bay and in Gower. There also seemed to be little in the way of seaside entertainment although I think I had a donkey ride which scared me. I do remember that there was a black range type stove in the main room that seemed to be a combined kitchen living room that I was warned not to touch and it seemed very dark, maybe it was gas lit!

I believe Auntie Minnie's was on the riverbank in the above photo but I can't be sure.

Strangely some years later this scary holiday did not put me off spending a more pleasant three years there at university which with generous student grants, cheap drink and good company did seem more like a holiday but the beach was still disappointedly stoney!

Another holiday with relatives was to stay with one of my Mum's aunts in London. This was my first trip to the capital and I guess I was about nine or ten and it was the first opportunity to see the sights that were familiar from books, films and television. We were promised we would see the guards, Buckingham palace, the Tower of London and Beefeaters etc etc. I was excited about going on the London underground so that was definitely on my must do list. Years later, when on working visits to the capital, I would avoid the underground like the plague and opt to walk or take a cab! The journey must have been in the summer holidays and the car was packed the night before and the family was up at the crack of dawn and set off before breakfast stopping a couple of hours later for a picnic breakfast in at the roadside. This was the 1950's British road system and although sections of the M1 had been recently completed the Swansea to London route was the old A48, through Chepstow with the Severn Bridge crossing over the wide expanse of the Bristol Channel still in the planning stages. There were several other stops but not just for refreshments and breaks. My Dad still seemed to need to 'clean the plugs' on the car every couple of hours to stop the misfiring so all in all the 'adventure' took the entire time of a summer's daylight hours. I believe we didn't arrive until after dark about ten thirty in London, or more correctly in Woodford Green, Essex, so north east London. We were welcomed by my great aunt and her two sons who although they were my Mum's cousins were both between my age and my parents. My brother and myself went straight to bed but were promised that Derek and Robin would play cricket and take us fishing and kite flying. I guess it was next morning that we set off to see the sights unless my Dad had a rest day locally after what must have been a tiring drive punctuated by amateur car engine maintenance!

Initially on the sightseeing I experienced a major disappointment. We entered the London Underground station in Woodford and after taking our seats on our train I was shocked when it emerged from the station to find we could still see trees and houses. My brother and me both exclaimed "This isn't underground ! It's just like a normal train!" The next few stops were spent somewhat grumpily while we waited for my Dad's promise that we would be going underground to be fulfilled. Of course he was right - although the noise of the trains amplified in the tunnel I found rather unpleasant and I was pleased to get out. I also didn't approve of the rickety wooden escalators that didn't seem as smooth as the smaller more modern ones we had infrequently encountered in department stores at home or in Cardiff. Still we were out on the London streets and it did seem busier and more crowded than towns of our previous experience.

Over the next few days my parents were as good as their word and we visited all the promised sights . We must have walked our socks off. The Crown Jewels, Beefeaters and Ravens were all seen at the Tower. At that time there was no shuffling past the display cases and we could ogle the jewels at our leisure - different times. We crossed the Thames and saw Tower Bridge as well as Hampton Court on a trip up the river. We ate in Lyons Corner House with the 'nippy' waitresses in their uniforms, much posher than the upstairs Woolworths cafeteria at home. We visited the big shops in Oxford street amazed by their size, and window shopped in the Burlington arcade. I guess we went to Liberty's as I remember a Tudor style building. Years later it became my favourite London store particularly as my designer wife had some textiles stocked and sold there. A mark of her talent as a designer which made me extremely proud of her.

One day we couldn't wait to get back to tell Aunt Ivy of a stroke of luck that had occurred. When walking down the Mall to see Buckingham Palace we saw a police escort of outriders coming down the road slowly with horse guards and a coach with the Queen waving as she went past accompanied by amongst others a lady in brightly coloured clothes. We later found out it was the state visit of the King and Queen of Thailand. My Dad claimed it was especially arranged for us but we didn't believe him.

The visit to the capital certainly met my expectations and I have never really lost the slight sense of awe at the bustle of activity in the city. Many years later I spent days there for business and went to places I couldn't imagine at nine years of age. Several such experiences come to mind. The first is going with my school friend Jack for lunch when we both were at meetings in the city and enjoying a good lunch near the Houses of Parliament and as the bill arrived both of us offering to pick it up and charge our expense accounts. We had a laugh and said who would have expected that two Sketty schoolboys would find themselves in that position some forty years later !

The second experience near the end of my career in industry was finding myself getting out of a cab and walking into the offices of a merchant bank with a set of documents to finalise the sale of the company I worked for from its US owners to a European company for some billion and a half pounds. I wasn't even getting a percentage !

On the trip to London we had looked up at the statue of Nelson atop his column in Trafalgar Square I was not to

suspect that one day I would put my hand on Nelsons head! I knew one of the directors of the company that was contracted to clean and renovate the column and statues in the square. I was working in an advisory capacity with them on business planning. They had scaffolding up the column and a platform at the top around the statue where the cleaning was being done.

Before our meeting that afternoon in the more hospitable surroundings of the Institute of Directors I was invited to take a trip to the top of the column to see Nelson. I am not a great fan of heights but when I was told that fewer than thirty people had been up there including the mayor of London and the Blue Peter film crew it was hard to miss the opportunity. I have photo of me in a hard hat with a nervous expression and my hand on Nelson's hat with the National Gallery looking like a matchbox below. As I pressed nervously on the stone of the head, probably trying to cool my hand and lower my blood pressure I rather alarmed my guide by saying "it feels as if something is moving!"

The swift answer was " I hope it's only you or the bloody scaffold platform." So thank you Adrian but it's not something I want to repeat so don't order the scaffolding just for me.

Although the trip to London was exciting and the fourteen hour car journey was certainly memorable of equal impact and certainly causing a greater degree of anticipation was our first holiday in a Butlin's holiday camp!

In the 1950's to working families or at least to the children this was akin to a trip to the Seychelles, only with funfair rides. The experience has crept back into the public conscience through the TV series 'Hi-de-Hi" and from memory it seemed to recreate at least some of the experience with some accuracy. It was in the summer holidays when I was six approaching seven and my brother was three years younger. Some classmates had already been and came back with tales of unlimited free fairground rides, talent shows and games, large swimming lidos and glamorous theatres and ballrooms where children were allowed in for milk shakes and lemonades and ice cream sundaes. It all sounded too good to be true. And where was this extravaganza for the senses to take place ? - the hard to pronounce North Wales resort of Pwllheli ! I am not sure if we travelled there by coach or car but I guess it seemed a long journey to an eager six year old.

Family photographs of the holiday show my brother and me bizarrely wearing cowboy hats in most of them - cowboys were big in the 1950's due to the pervasive influence of post war American culture on our TV and cinema screens. How many of us recall the names of such western heroes as the Cisco kid, the Lone Ranger (or Kemosabe) as he was known to
his native Indian and somewhat downtrodden sidekick (read a sort of buckskin butler) named Tonto. He was played by a Canadian actor by the glorious name of Jay Silverheels who research tells me was a star lacrosse player in his pre-buckskin days. The masked Lone Ranger seems to display more affection for his white horse -"Silver,' and many days Tonto must have yearned a return to the more egalitarian world of lacrosse. But other interesting conjecture exists around the relationship of these two with the suggestion that as Tonto in Spanish translates as 'stupid' or 'crazy' the term 'kemosabe'

means 'idiot' in Apache. Whatever the truth was they had more glamorous and credible names than Hopalong Cassidy clearly some early attempt at an equal opportunities hero.
I digress, there are other photos of us sitting in and steering small cars around a track, still wearing cowboy hats. In rowing boats, on model railways, electric rocking horses and what appears to be a not very realistic but full sized mechanical elephant One of the amazing observations is that at Butlins I appear to be wearing a collar and tie - with the cowboy hat. My brother is more equinely authentic wearing a set of reins, very fashionable in the 1950's for child control and probably outlawed now under the Geneva convention. The accommodation was certainly not luxurious and would appear very regimented in more recent times. Some of the camps were converted barracks and the 'chalets,' think terraced wooden single storey huts, they were very accurately portrayed in 'Hi-de-Hi.'

One attraction to parents was the presence of chalet maid patrols at night so that the parents could leave their children for the evening and go to a film or variety show safe in the knowledge that the patrolling maids would call the on the tannoy if they were needed. Unfortunately this was to happen to my parents when their visit to a show was interrupted by a call for the residents of chalet X were asked to return to attend to their children. My Mum would recall the incident, (all to frequently for my liking,) that upon returning to the chalet they found a small crowd outside accompanying the chalet patrol who were shining a torch through the window at me sitting on the floor, bawling my eyes out and nursing a nasty bite on my arm inflicted by my brother during some argument over positioning in the bunk beds. Photos of other activities during the holiday suggest the feud was forgotten but I don't know how many more evenings out my parents enjoyed that holiday.

I mention earlier how summer holidays in those days were often spent with relatives and it was also the case that if the annual holiday destination was near to or en route for any old acquaintances or family members living away from us the opportunity was not missed to see them. This was not as if childhood did not already have enough tea times at relatives houses being told how much you had grown and answering mild interrogations about what you had learned at school. And you were meant to be on holiday for goodness sake and having a rest from the rigours of learning. Nevertheless, there could be bonuses like the brief period of rabbit ownership following a visit to Uncle Jim's in Wiltshire. On a later holiday in either Bournemouth or the New Forest we visited my Mum's Auntie Lilly not very memorable in itself, but it must have been prearranged as she mentioned that her son, my Mum's cousin, was at home from sea and had asked if we had time during our holiday to be shown over his ship. It was readily agreed that this would happen the next day and although it was exciting my parents had kept from my brother and myself the name of the ship. Living in Swansea with a busy docks at that time it was not exactly unusual for guided tours of ships in port and in my childhood we took regular tours of ships in dock, usually on Sunday afternoon and we had seen frigates, destroyers, minesweepers and submarines as well as some merchant ships. Perhaps my Dad was reliving his seagoing youth but probably not the Dunkirk evacuation.

That morning we drove into Southampton docks in our family Morris Traveller, I am sure security was more lax in those days. We walked down the quayside to be towered over by a huge shape with multiple gangplanks and uncle Frank waiting at the bottom of one. "Welcome to the Queen Mary - come aboard" It was one of the biggest things I had ever seen and dwarfed the town buildings at home in Swansea. I didn't know what position Frank held aboard, he certainly wasn't the captain but in his smart pressed uniform and his acknowledgment by the few members of the crew we met he made us feel as important as any time in my life previously. We were shown some of the cabins, large plush ones and smaller ones and his laughter when I asked him whether his quarters aboard were like that was quite telling. My strongest memory was of the indoor tiled swimming pool and the small street of shops on two levels with a wide staircase

joining them. It was soon time to leave but it was certainly the highlight of the holiday for me.

My parents were diligent in our education away from school so we visited castles, museums and historic sites both from home and when on holiday. Arriving at Stonehenge not long after dawn following a night time journey isn't something you forget in a hurry and my Dad was quick to tell us that it was thought the stones themselves had arrived from the Prescellli mountains in Pembrokeshire so we felt some regional pride in the site. In those days the stones weren't fenced off so they could be walked around and touched - more trusting and relaxed times or a better behaved public? We also visited Glastonbury Tor and Avebury but to my shame I was more impressed by the model village at Bourton on the Water and debated with my Dad at home over the feasibility of some limited recreation in our small suburban garden using shoe boxes as moulds and cement as he always seemed to have half a bag of it, (going slowly solid) in the corner of the garage. It never happened but it was a childhood dream.

I mentioned earlier that the family were temporary owners of a static caravan on a site in North Gower. It came to us by way of my Mum's brother Arthur who was something of a childhood hero of mine being an army captain as well as the source of parcels of exotic items sent to us from his postings overseas. He died tragically early I believe of long term health complications having been a prisoner of war in a Japanese prison camp.

We only kept the caravan for one year but it provided joyful escapes at weekends and school holidays. Years later we acquired on of a similar size and vintage for our garden in Sussex which was used as my wife's studio and a 1950's personal vintage museum. Caravan breaks were wonderful as after a cooked breakfast my Dad drove back to Swansea if he was at work. Along with my brother and with a friend who might be staying we would head to the beach through the sand dunes accompanied by the dog under instructions to return for lunch. We joined up with other groups of children and played games of football or cricket on the beach. Rock pools were explored and the beach combed for treasures, normally odd pieces of driftwood or shells - I don't recall any valuable discoveries. There was the constant need to deter Patch from sticking his nose in a washed up dogfish or jelly fish. Caterpillars were collected in jam-jars in the dunes - it was a Famous Five style of adventure without the sail boat or improbable encounters with pirates or gangsters.
Caravan living is like life in miniature with everything to hand or under your feet depending on your mood. I think the caravan had a series of rooms that were created by folding screens there was sink and a cooker but I don't recall a fridge but wouldn't have noticed one and food could be bought daily in the shop on the site. The toilet / bathroom facilities were in a shower block on the campsite. I don't know if there was any electricity, most probably there were gas mantle lights - all very retro.
I don't know whether it preceded the caravan or whether it was a by-product of my Dad's time in the sea scouts and later in the army but he was an enthusiast of camping stoves. These were normally used to boil a kettle for cups of tea possibly after one of the frequent impromptu roadside

car repairs. Occasionally some soup might be heated for us to all drink out of bakelite mugs.

One of these outdoor gourmet experiences was the subject of an early and rare success in the world of writing. We were asked in school, somewhat ambitiously in retrospect, by our class teacher, Miss Sharpe, to write on the subject of Our Best Day. I don't know what the rest of the class of seven and eight year olds wrote. Tales of birthdays, Christmas or trips to funfairs or maybe a day at a Butlins holiday camp. I was rather embarrassed to be called out in front of the class to read my masterpiece out in probably one of my first spoken public appearances. So no doubt with my ears glowing bashfully I read out my account of a recent day trip out to a river near Llandeilo with my Mum and Dad when my brother and I fished in the water with nets and jam jars for minnows before enjoying a fry up of eggs, bacon, sausages and fried bread cooked in a frying pan on my Dad's stove. I do remember it then and now as a beautiful day out and I now realise that my teacher had recognised and appreciated the joy in simple pleasures and wished to celebrate it. Perhaps for me it was the first time that a piece of my writing was appreciated so I thank her for that.

Scouts

I believe the first night I spent away from home by myself, (apart from the memorable hospital stay for the tonsils op!) was my first scout camp. This would be at the age of eleven and over the Whitsun half term and for some three or four nights in the exotic setting of Parc Le Breos valley, Parkmill in Gower.

The extract from a larger photo shows myself with three other desperados that I hope they won't mind me identifying as Dr Mike Thomas, Jack Jones CBE, and Robert Thomas ex Monash University.

The freedom of scout camp was a revelation and obviously gave us a grounding for future career success.
At the time the ability to stay awake as long as you liked, wash infrequently, eat smoky greasy fried food in vast

quantities supplemented by stockpiles of chocolate, sweets and biscuits from the village shop were of greater appeal to us. Supplemented by the ability to play with fire and axes and sharp knives made for an idyllic few days for eleven year old boys. This was only marginally offset by having to dig a hole to use as a toilet and to wash, (infrequently) in cold water. The valley sides at Parc Le Brios are carpeted with wild garlic and it was this strong smell coupled with us and all our clothes smelling exclusively of fried food and woodsmoke that must have tempered my parents joy to be reunited with me at home after only four days. This was particularly true in my case as my father professed a pathological hatred of onions and garlic -particularly their smell.

There was some order to the camp as the Scout movement seems to be founded on semi-military foundations. Tents were I believe 'Nijers' made of thick green canvas with a bell end at the back and two wooden poles that were as thick as your arm. They were high enough for us to stand up in the centre at the ridge. Patrols slept six or seven to a tent with some storage behind the rear pole at the bell end. There was a separate ground sheet and the side panels could be rolled up around a foot and a half for airing. This was I recall referred to as braiding the tent and each morning at camp, unless it was raining, our kit was placed on our individual ground sheets in a line outside the tent with our spare clothes and belongings neatly laid out for kit inspection by the scout leaders. This was an opportunity to air the tent - pretty essential if half a dozen boys had been sleeping in there after a diet of fried food and copious helpings of eggs and baked beans.

I recall that one at one camp there was an outbreak of enthusiasm for pickled onions and supplies were brought along and supplemented with additional purchases of more jars bought from a nearby shop, along with ginger beer and dandelion and burdock. This was before the later onset of more mature tastes such as beer and cider. Lord knows what this did for the digestion and the airing of the tent must have been a great relief. The daily inspection gave an air of organisation to the camp but considering the relative lack of supervision and the abundance of fire and sharp weaponry the absence of frequent trips to a hospital was remarkable. Perhaps there was a reluctance to experience first aid treatment from your half trained (and possibly half-brained) fellow scout troop members that held the danger just back a hair's breadth from a visit to accident and emergency.

As if there wasn't enough excitement to be created in daylight and I include in this the popular game of 'Stretch.' To describe this as foolhardy is a massive understatement. The game consisted of two participants standing facing each other some six foot apart and with their feet together. Each would have a sheath knife (basically a dagger,) which they would throw to stick in the ground at the side of the opponent's foot but maybe 6 or 9 inches away. The receiver would then stretch their leg to touch the knife and then throw their own knife to 'stretch' the opponent. The idea was to stretch the game by small increments in movement and heighten tension with the proximity of the landing area to an already outstretched foot. The victor was the one left standing but flesh wounds were an immediate dis-

qualification. Given that the preferred footwear around the camp were wellies or plimsoles, depending on the weather, with hiking boots reserved for offsite and trainers yet to be invented you can see that the footwear offered very limited protection.

Amazingly I can't recall any injuries to feet although one or two pierced wellington toe caps were cited as narrow escapes and usually resulted in the leaders banning the game for the remainder of the camp. The suggestion of enlivening the activity by deploying hand axes was also refused as not in the spirit of the game.

The other thing that needed banning on occasions was gambling -this was low level stuff and ranged from informal bets such as 'I bet you can't throw the washing up bowl right across the river,' to long games of pontoon or 21 into the night or on wet tent bound afternoons. The stakes were pennies but serious hustlers could make inroads into the weeks spending money of the less experienced gamblers.

An additional danger provided at camps was the aerial runway. Often the campsites were in valleys and this was true of the first camp I went on in Parkmill. The valley sides allowed the construction of an aerial runway by stretching a taut rope between trees or a tripod set on the valley floor from long boughs cut from trees. With some vague nod to health and safety I have been reminded some fifty years after the event by a fellow scout that the younger scouts were only allowed to use the smaller hand axes with the long two handed felling axes to only be wielded by the older scouts when felling trees!

To construct the runway a pulley was fixed to the rope with a bar strung below it to hang onto to then slide down the slope of the rope. Speed could be increased by greasing the rope and pulley. Theoretically the speed could be controlled by a brake rope attached to the pulley and held at the top of the run by a 'brake man' to slow the descent but the flaw in this safety feature can be easily spotted by anyone used to dealing with teenage boys. Sometimes the stop at the bottom of the run was sudden enough to cause the 'pilot' to lose their grip and fly off to land on the ground. Again it seemed miraculous that regular visits to the local A and E department were not required.

As I was saying further excitement at camp could be had during the hours of darkness - the fires were stoked up and producing random sparks to alight on people sitting nearby (mercifully mostly wearing natural materials as man-made fibres were not so ubiquitous then.) Lighting was by paraffin hurricane lamps or pressurised Tilley lamps, brighter but the subject of urban myth stories of being prone to exploding so I always kept my distance from them and there was the camp highlight of the Wide Game. I am hazy about the actual process and in particular about the rules, if there were any. Probably on the last night of the camp and after dark the troop was divided into two teams and the first one given a start to some distant objective. The first one I remember would have been in Parkmill when we were to make our way to the castle above Three Cliffs Bay by way of Parkmill valley. As an eleven year old not long from having the landing light on for sleeping at home this was rather exciting and a little bit intimidating. The drama was heightened by some of the older scouts outside the two teams ambushing both teams with fireworks and flour bombs. Quite why no-one fell in the stream there or broke their ankles in the darkness only relieved by our rather inadequate hand torches is a miracle. Still the event was unanimously agreed the next day to have been the highlight of the camp apart from one keen junior anthropologist who announced it a failure because he hadn't seen any nocturnal wild animals. Clearly his amateur studies hadn't yet developed sufficiently to inform him that any nocturnal animal may have been rather alert to the presence of some thirty boisterous scouts blundering about by torchlight and have swiftly legged it!

Cooking was over wood fires which had the benefit of keeping us occupied gathering firewood this limiting time spent on more dangerous activities such as 'stretch' or aerial runways. The downside was it made us and all our clothes smell of woodsmoke but maybe it disguised the wild garlic smell. As well as frying there were large pans called 'dixies' used for boiling potatoes and whatever other vegetables we could be persuaded to eat. The potatoes were often used along with onions and tinned of corned beef to make corned beef hash, quite a favourite of mine. Sitting around the campfire I don't remember toasted marshmallows, (maybe this was a later transatlantic import.)

I do recall a plainer version we called 'twists.' The were simply a length of flour and water paste twisted around a stick and cooked over the flames, or most likely partially cooked as the outside would be toasted brown to black while the inside was still doughy. They could be enlivened with a coating of syrup or jam. The other innovation was the biscuit tin oven which involved placing food inside a large caterers square biscuit tin on top of a fire pit and covering the top with earth clods. I don't really remember any gourmet roast dinners emerging from these but I do remember my friend Bruce incurring the wrath of my mother. I had returned home from camp and unpacking she discovered one of her prized enamel cooking bowls which had been lent to me was missing a large proportion of it's enamel. I explained my alibi that Bruce had borrowed it to combine the 'twist' with the biscuit tin oven to bake a bread roll, unsuccessfully as it had burned to crisp and removed the enamel from the bowl. I advised him to avoid our house for a few days.

Over the years and a few years older further scout camps were to follow including my first trips abroad but this was all in the future.

Playing

Living in South Wales much of my play was carried on indoors particularly in the early years. But as Swansea is blessed with number of parks within walking distance of our house as well as sandy beaches a walk or bus ride away visits to both with my parents were an enjoyable part of my of my early life. Family photos show sandcastles and fishing nets on the beach, games of cricket and kite flying as well as scooters and bikes. At home we had a garden to play in and there was a lane at the back of the houses that could be used as an extension of the garden under instructions to go no further than the distance my Mum's voice could call us in for lunch or tea. The lane bordered a chapel at the back that was in the process of building a new church hall that seemed to be a slow process but the base foundations made for a solid surface for ball games for several months. The top end of the lane backed onto the school playground below. There were still two flat roofed air-raid shelters near the wall and bigger boys were seen leaping across the gap to climb on the roof. I don't recall ever doing this but some late afternoons it was still possible to play football in the playground after school and to be close enough that Mum could call me home from the top of the garden or the lane. Further down the lane was the back of a large garden of a house in the next road which had a big mature spreading tree on its border with low branches that we could climb on. There was a slightly older boy who sometimes came there and showed us that the tree had masses of small hard fruit. I remember it giving us ample ammunition to throw at each other which was fine until later in the year when it ripened and messed up our hair and clothes as the tree was fig tree. I can't recall eating them although we were quite experienced at chewing clover and blackberries and any apples we found out and about. There was also a fibrous cane type plant which tasted lemony and we called 'gypsy rhubarb' which doubled as swords and ad hoc refreshment. Further down the lane bordered a large cemetery which was home to lizards and slow-worms and also rather popular with the cats of the neighbourhood. We avoided using it as playground other than the occasional wildlife hunting expedition and using it for a short cut to friends houses that were across from it. In my last two years in junior school a church hall in the cemetery was used as an overflow classroom but we were marched from the school in a crocodile from assembly and at breaks to it from the main school. It can't have done our studies any harm as virtually the whole of the class of some forty plus boys and girls passed the eleven plus and went on to grammar schools. Maybe the exercise stimulated our brain cells.

Visits to cemeteries were more frequent for families then maybe because burials were more common than cremation and also extended families stayed in the same area. I don't know how often we visited Oystermouth cemetery but I believe a number of relatives on my father's side of the family are buried there. I suspect it was an annual visit for an anniversary of a death or perhaps a birthday but much more significant to me at a young age was an impressive trick my Dad performed. I guess it must have been in the autumn or winter as my father was wearing his trilby hat. Hat wearing is a lost art today and was much more commonplace amongst adults then.

Personally I have a theory that the abandonment of it in later years has contributed to the outbreak of young male baldness but it may be due to central heating, overuse of hair products as a teenager or exposure to cathode ray tube emissions through prolonged tv viewing. I am currently favouring hair products as although I briefly experimented with Brylcream hair grease in the early 1960'S the coming of the Beatles and long unkempt hair put an end to this experiment and I have not seriously dabbled in male hair grooming products since. I am pleased to say I have a full and luxuriant head of hair still.

Back to the cemetery. As we walked up the path we were surprised to see a hedgehog walk across the path some twenty yards in front of us. Our surprise was amplified by my Dad's action, perhaps as a result of seeing too many cowboy films, when in one swift movement he removed his trilby hat and threw it, Frisbee style in a straight line to drop on top of the hedgehog. This was amazing on a number of levels.

Firstly, the Frisbee had yet to make its way to Britain, Secondly, it seemed an impulsive reaction not typical of my Dad. Lastly, why had he done this and what was he planning to do with the captured quarry.

Shortly afterwards having examined the hedgehog that had now rolled up into a prickly ball and had to be gently released into the nearest hedge I think my Dad was trying to answer question three whilst scratching his head. I can only conclude he wasn't paying attention when people gave out 'important facts to remember about hedgehogs.' Fact one they are painful to pick up so use something material for this to avoid being spiked. Fact two - if this preferred material is your hat, never, NEVER put it back on your head because - as Dad discovered - hedgehogs are covered in fleas - so is your hat and now - so is your head. I think we rapidly went home to wash my Dad's hair. Still, all in all, a lesson learned and I have subsequently avoided any hedgehog, flea, hat combinations!

Gradually my horizons were broadened and it wasn't uncommon for children of eight years old and upwards to be walking alone to nearby friends houses under instructions to "go straight there, take care crossing the roads." Local roads in any event were virtually devoid of traffic to the extent that ad hoc games of football or cricket could be played in the side roads with only the occasional interruption by a rare passing car or van. I have already mentioned that the local library was deemed to be 'within safe range' and as time went on other locations were added to my approved destinations. In those days local shops often delivered so it wasn't uncommon for children to be despatched to the grocers, or butchers with a shopping list for a later delivery and with luck clutching a thruppenny bit or even a sixpence 'for going.' This could be spent in the neighbouring sweetshop or the newsagents. Thinking back within some two or three hundred yards from our house there was a wealth of shops of greater or lesser interest to me. The local shops also provided other ancillary services. Firstly, there was the local gossip. Any local information, positive of otherwise would be readily provided in the local shop if not by the shopkeeper themselves then by other customers, first

or second hand. Of course the information may not always be strictly accurate and there was always the danger of congratulating the wrong Mrs Jones on her daughter's engagement etc and could lead to confusion.
Another service provided in our community was a kind of informal medical triage where the local chemist, Mr Jones, could be consulted on medical matters to avoid all the tedious hanging around in the doctor's waiting room. We also deployed a secondary route by asking a friend of Mum's, Mrs Lulu Evans, who ran the corner shop opposite and had previously worked as a nurse. These were more reliable ways of getting advice in those days rather than today's 'Googling' of symptoms which usually leads you to doubt you will see the day out!

Of most interest to me were the sweetshops of which amazingly there were three! It explains the legacy of tooth decay suffered by post-war generations with their enthusiasm spurred on by the removal of sugar and sweet rationing.
The range of sugary treats was astonishing - the wrapped range of sweets, some of which still exist today, (I say they do - I take a limited interest now as I am anxious to avoid any further dentistry,)
but I believe Polos, Smarties, Rollos and the range of chocolate bars have survived. Of more interest to us connoisseurs of confectionary were the penny or four for a penny loose sweets that were more exciting - long strings of liquorish, Trebor sherbets, rice paper flying saucers, or pink shrimps and yellow sweet bananas. There was always the option of choosing two or four ounces, known popularly as a quarter, of the loose sweets from large glass sweet jars. The advantage here was that a kindly assistant would often pop an additional couple of sweets into the scales scoop after the weighing. This was much appreciated and a popular topic of discussion when choosing which sweet shop should be graced with our patronage.

I later became a little squeamish about these jars after a kindly owner provided me with an empty one to raise my

tadpoles in after we called into the shop carrying a haul of captured tadpoles in a small jam-jar when returning from the park. Certainly any liquorish delights in these sweet jars had completely lost their appeal to me after that.

The other lunacy, and I can't believe I am writing this, was that sweet manufacturers produced a range of sweet cigarettes, pipes, sweet tobacco and matches that allowed children to start out on the slippery slope of nicotine addiction (and all the associated health hazards therein), at an early age. That is always assuming they didn't perish by starting a house fire through the escalation from sweet matches to the real thing. Oh yes, we lived in risky times!

Of almost as much interest as the sweetshops were the newsagents as they sold sweets and lemonade along with their supply of comics and small toys such as toy gliders or model kits. Shops that supplied grocery deliveries were attractive because of the pocket money earning potential although I preferred the grocers to the butchers where whole carcasses and gruesome pigs heads or whole chickens, rabbits and pheasants were on display. The grocers were more clinical with the meat having been processed into sausages, pies or sliced ham thus disguising their origins for the more squeamish.

The ironmongers has some limited interest as the display was intriguing and it was a source of batteries for toys.

There were other shops such as the greengrocers, chemists, knitting shop and ladies hairdressers that were of no interest to me. It was also some time before the joys of the contents of the off-licence were of personal interest. My parents weren't regular customers either with the Christmas bottle of sherry or port lingering in the house for most of the year. Although I do recall the off-licence was the source of the orange bottles of Lucozade that was only bought when someone was under the weather and came with satisfactorily expensive orange crinkly cellophane wrapping that demanded incorporation into home made spaceman or divers helmets. I am unsure of any scientific proof of the curative properties of Lucozade but it made missing school and being confined to bed with some minor ailment for a day or two slightly more bearable as fizzy drinks were considered a luxury product for most in the 1950's rather than a regular purchase. Comparing notes with contemporaries I find I wasn't the only child that would 'improvise a home made beverage' combining orange squash with a spoonful of Andrews liver salts from the medicine cupboard.

Play in other friends gardens was replaced before the age of eleven by roaming locally to less supervised areas including the local parks.

The largest is Singleton park, a large park of over 200 acres, originally the estate owned by the Vivian family who were copper industrialists owning the works in the lower Swansea valley. Their house is now part of Swansea university which together with the hospital occupies the southern part of the park. The park is mostly grassland broken up by many mature trees. A small stream runs along one of the borders that was used to sail down sticks and leaves. The stream was a source of mystery as the constant flow of water left the park and flowed under the Mumbles road onto the beach but it started in the park down from the top north western corner, emerging from a large pipe. This must have come under the road at the top park entrance but the likely source was a similar sized stream over a mile to the north running in the valley between Tycoch and Cockett in an area we knew as the Griag.
Within Singleton park were some separate areas. At the top of the park behind Sketty Church was the 'Vicarage Field'

used for church fetes and also by the Sketty Cubs pack that I had joined. In the northwest top corner was the grammar school I was to go to from the age of eleven. Other areas in the park were the Educational gardens, home to herbaceous borders and nursery greenhouses as well as interesting rockeries and shrubberies. The complex of screened paths were attractive to small boys for rowdy games of tag and hide and seek. No doubt to the annoyance of adults who were merely trying to enjoy the horticultural splendours there. Another separate area we called the Rhododendron garden again a network of paths between taller shrubs with the added benefit of some kind of stone folly ramparts incorporating some stone grottoes all very useful for boyhood games of imaginative jungle adventures. We were so fortunate to have these and several other parks all within less than a half hours walk from home. Also at that time, five minutes walk away, was the Griag a small hillside area mostly full of fern and bracken and in the other direction was Hendrefoilan woods with what must have been a bomb crater that could be swung over on rope swings attached to the bordering trees.

Of my circle of friends in junior school around ten of them lived less than half a mile away, some just down the road. Martyn and Andrew were in the same road; Robert just around the corner towards the library; Jack and Bruce in houses up the hill opposite, Roger, Mike and John in roads just down from the shops in the square and Vernon just up another hill near the woods we played in. Most of them also attended sunday school or cubs and all of us lived within a ten minute walk of each other. We went to each others birthday parties, played at each others houses and gardens and were allowed a certain amount of freedom to walk to cubs together or to the local parks and playgrounds.

There wasn't the technology safety net of mobiles or in many cases landlines. The dialogue was usually along the lines of "who are you going with? Be back by a time or for lunch / tea." Parents usually knew one another and the roads were so much quieter so traffic was much less of a danger.

The range of our adventures was to expand from around the age of eleven once two wheel bikes were acquired. Traffic on the roads was at a much lower volume so even at that age we were allowed the freedom to cycle to beach and along to Mumbles as well as into Gower. My parents insisted that I took the cycling proficiency badge which was conducted over a series of evenings in the playground of Sketty school in Tycoch. I don't remember much of the detail of this other than being encouraged to weave on the bike between a line of orange plastic cones. This is something I don't remember requiring on the actual road but I guess it encouraged some limited mastery of accurate steering. Despite our young age and limited training for the hazards of the road we always rode on the road, not the pavements. All bikes had bells and hand signals were regularly used. The only accident I can recall was when one of my friends had his bike knocked over as we were in a line pushing our bikes up the hill from Caswell and a red sports car lost control coming around the bend too fast. The car's tail slid sideways knocking over the bike and Roger with it. When he stopped the driver was more concerned about the chunk of fibreglass that had being gouged out of the wing by Roger's bike pedal. We recognised him as our head boy at Bishop Gore school who as well as owning a red sports car had a double barrelled surname and was regarded already by us as a snob and something of a prize prat. I don't recall the outcome or whether there was damage to the bike and whether it was paid for but I do remember accusations being made along the lines of whose fault it was and 'we know who you are,' being darkly offered.

Despite the limited options for entertainment it seems in retrospect to be a golden age to be a child. Through the NHS and inoculation programmes serious childhood illness appeared a rarity and compared with earlier generations we seemed well fed and comfortable. I am sure to modern generations clothing would seem limited and our diets were more restricted but I guess we were more active.
I realise this section is titled Playing and I have digressed somewhat from the subject so let me put that right below.

Games

They can be split in my memory between outdoor games and indoor which were predominantly but not always board games. Before the age of eleven and secondary school the

outdoor games were in the main improvised. Such anarchy included games of tag and a variation called 'Release' when the tagged victim was brought back to a 'jail' where they could be freed or released hence the name by a free runner. If the game had a solitary catcher it could go on for ages until boredom or exhaustion set in so, if the total players were enough, multiple catchers or jailers could be deployed which was more likely in a school playground rather than when five or six of us were out playing after school or in the holidays. My brother and his group of friends were able to further complicate matters and dispute decisions as his class had two sets of identical twin boys, the Evans twins and the

Davies twins, (this was Wales after all.) Both sets were not above claiming to be one another; I mean each in their set of twins - you can see how confusing it is without even seeing them.

Playground games of football tended to be a mass of small boys against one goalie defending the gap between two uprights of the playground shelter though there were sometimes attempts to improvise a second set of goals and divide up into roughly equal teams. Cricket was similarly unstructured and something known bizarrely as 'French cricket' consisted of a batsman defending his legs as a substitute wicket against underarm bowling from whoever had the ball. (No wonder the French have not emerged as a premier nation in the world of cricket!)

Another anachronism was that Junior school, unlike the infants, had segregated playgrounds for girls and boys so that the boys were not corrupted by unseemly games of skipping or hopscotch. It was no wonder that for most of my youth the female sex seemed somewhat mysterious and unfathonable to me.

Board games were very popular in my youth and the predominance of wet weather in South Wales certainly helped in their popularity. Apart from draughts, chess and monopoly there was Cluedo and some Treasure Hunt game involving pirate ships that may have been called Buccaneer. For longer wet afternoons there was the game of Risk that seemed to take hours and involved capturing countries on a world map like a miniature cardboard and less repressive version of what the 18th and 19th century European nations had carried out for real. There was a game of miniature football known as 'Subbuteo' that I remember playing at a friends house and I also remember it being singularly tedious. You set up your two teams of little plastic footballers that had solid curved half globe weighted bases. You then took it in turns to flick these at an improbably out of scale plastic football with the objective of scoring in one of the small plastic nets. With any luck the ball was lost or stolen by the resident cat or dog before tedium set in, usually under ten minutes for me. I have subsequently heard of a rarer variation in the form of a cricket match but I was never unfortunate to know anyone who had a set or the requisite patience five days to play it for days on end as that seems to be the time span for that sport.

There was a more exciting and less OCD game, known as blow or table football where opponents would propel a light small plastic football towards a small net at either end of the improvised pitch on a table top. As the name suggests propulsion was provided by blowing through a straw and although quite exciting and entertaining I am sure it was an excellent way of spreading childhood germs around.

Plus someone, probably your mother had to wipe the table down before mealtime which can't have been very hygienic. There were attempts as educational games but I have difficulty in remembering many of them. I imagine there must have been quiz cards with the chance to recall the longest river of highest building etc. I do remember one called accurately "Tell Me" which attempted to dramatise the format by having a kind of spinning wheel to select the letter of the alphabet that had to be used to tell the name of an item on the card selected that was spelt with that letter e.g a flower or a tree. I suppose it could demonstrate some rudimentary general knowledge but I am not surprised that later generations welcomed Sonic the Hedgehog and subsequent computer games so readily.

One educational game that was briefly astonishing, at least for the first five minutes was "The Amazing Magic Robot Quiz Game" In this there was a series of circular card inserts of questions with a 3d model robot quizmaster with a pointer. You would dial his wand around to the question to be answered then move him across to the centre of the answers where he would be placed on a mirrored centre - here he would spin around to point his wand at the correct answer. Initially it was impressive until it dawned on the audience that the answers and questions we arranges around the circle in consecutive order and you were dialling some circular magnetic mechanism below to synchronise the question and answer. Still the slow of understanding were intrigued for a while and I have witnessed less entertaining episodes of Mastermind on tedious trivia, like Puddings of the World and the Socks of the Royal family.

Toys were similarly relatively unsophisticated although the lack of battery power in the main must have been a relief to fathers of that generation. Cars were mostly push along, clockwork or 'friction' a sort of flywheel accelerated push along. My first and only train set was a Hornby clockwork one, a simple oval track if I remember correctly and quite large scale not HO and the coal tender large enough for outings for Hammy the hamster. A lot safer for him than the 12 volt train set my brother had later which would regularly give the dog a mild shock when he put his wet nose on the track which he did at regular intervals for some reason, possibly to enliven the tedium of life when he wasn't out for walks.

I saved my pocket money and birthday postal orders towards accessories for this train set which were buildings and bridges constructed of painted tin plate which was alarmingly sharp at the corners and not something you would want to fall heavily onto.

Around the same time one of the toy manufacturers produced a scale model road set compatible with the OO electric train sets. From what I can recall this was a less exciting version of the Scalextric car racing circuits and had cross roads and driveways into bungalows with up and over doors. Maybe it was less labour intensive than the fast racing cars which always seemed to need to be put back on the track after every other bend. In the relatively recent post war days it wasn't unusual for boys to have collections of toy soldiers and military vehicles so that a battle field scene could be set up in what we called the 'front room' which had sofas and armchairs and a coffee table and was away from the activity of the living room next door. Cushions and pile of book would be used to create hills and valleys or sand dunes if it was a desert campaign and as I had a field marshal Montgomery this was appropriate. The soldiers were lined up and small cannons or field guns were used to fire small marbles or matchsticks - all very violent but great for six or seven year old boys. The battlefield was occasional decimated by a weapon of mass destruction in the form of the family cat passing through or Patch the dog inquisitively investigating for anything edible.

Thinking back our young minds were not bothered by such details as scale so armies of 'dwarf' soldiers would be 'straffed' by a three inch long toy fighter aeroplane or knocked over by a cannonball twice their height. I believe this was good training for us NOT to write to the TV pages in later life complaining pedantically about the incorrect model of the Routemaster bus being used in some period drama or other. As well as soldiers there were model cowboys and red indians, also knights in armour complete with a nice model fort with a drawbridge, portcullis and siege ladders. Play with the fort was no doubt helped by seeing television series such as Sir Lancelot and Ivanhoe. One innovation I do recall was an attempt by one toy maker, Britains I believe, with their Swoppet range to refresh the toy soldier market with small plastic models that had interchangeable parts and swivelled so the could change a pose. Arms could be removed and heads taken off or the torso split. Belts could be removed and weapons swapped so they were aptly named. I am not sure if the 'boffins' in their product development department or 'development arm' as I would like to think it was called had this benefit in mind but it made for a new level of carnage to be able to be created on our home battlefields with one armed survivors or disembodied heads and headless torsos. If only they had thought to include small plastic puddles of blood.

As the range included western as well as medieval figures it was possible to have knights in armour with featured head-dresses or cowboy hats. Armoured chest plates could be enlivened by fringed buckskin chap leggings. No longer did us boys have to envy the dressing up opportunities that girls had for their dolls. Of course the size of the pieces and their ease of removal meant that losses would occur regularly and random limbs would be found under furniture or more like hoovered up or chewed by the dog. Looking at the prices today that collectors are willing to pay for complete models these were expensive losses - proving there is a price to pay for unfettered armed conflict.

One Christmas I remember receiving a particularly spectacular model tank from my grand parents. It was quite large and heavy with a powerful clockworks motor driving the tracks allowing it to climb over the cushion defences crushing swoppet soldiers and conventional forces alike. This wasn't all, the tank was equipped with other features - a gun turret that swivelled from side to side while a gunners head popped up out of a hatch, another gun that gave out sparks from some kind of grindwheel device while the main gun puffed out smoke from some refillable reservoir of fine powder. Some days later I experimented with refilling it with flour much to my Mums annoyance as this was messier. I briefly tried talcum powder but the fragrant smell was overpowering and didn't seem very warlike. I guess the tank went the way of most wind up toys in those days when overenthusiastic key winding broke or jammed something in the mechanism. My Dad would patiently dismantle toys in a usually unsuccessful attempt to unjam it so it would work again. On more than one occasion this resulted in several feet of sharp edged sprung flat wire exploding from the innards and narrowly avoiding injuring bystanders. Still he was always game to try despite previous experiences. There was always some optimism in those days of toy designers that an electric motor or clockwork mechanic in a toy boat would not quickly rust or corrode if exposed, of all things, to water. You were often on safer ground with simple gliders launched by catapults of strong rubber bands. One holiday morning was almost ruined when after morning coffee in a park-side cafe I persuaded my parents to let me launch my new delta winged plastic glider within the safety of the park across the road . It was the maiden flight as it had been bought with some holiday money the evening before. Toy shops in tourist areas were often open early evening to cash in on children's holiday cash. In the park the plane soared impressively toward the centre before performing a confident 180 degree turn and leaving the park, crossing the road and crash landing on the awning of the cafe we had just left. My Dad returned there and they kindly lowered the awning for retrieval. I expect we were committed to morning coffee for the rest of our week in Bournemouth in gratitude but I doubt that the glider safely went back home with us. This was the age of flight and although it was some years before I took my first flight like most of us 1950's kids I was obsessed with flight and aeroplanes and later with space race. There were trips to air shows at the RAF base at St Athens and any rare sighting of a military plan in the Welsh skies led to a rush for the binoculars or toy telescope in a belated attempt to identify it, leading to arguments - "It was a Vulcan bomber," -"No it was too small - it must have been a Javelin." Identification skills were improved with the introduction of Airfix model aircraft kits where for pocket money prices a small box or bag containing numerous pieces of plastic which when glued together formed a scale model of an aircraft, (or car, tank or boat.) This is always assuming the detailed instructions could be followed but the results were usually successful although it was always best to ensure best tables cloths, adjacent furniture or best jumpers were not contaminated with the plastic cement which proved particularly difficult to remove. The completed model could be improved with the transfers provided and there were also instructions for painting the model although I rarely had the patience to paint them once the triumph of assembly was completed. This led to a sense of disappointment as at the end of the day the models were static and incapable of proper flight. At friend's houses and in toy shops I started taking an interest in larger balsa wood aircraft kits that promised the wonder of flight. it was clear that the pocket money Airfix kits were a sort of 'gateway drug' to more expensive commitments both in terms of money and energy. Given that the larger balsa models were to take several months pocket money I approached purchase cautiously and even undertook some research. This included a visit to a friend's house to witness the much anticipated inaugural flight of a propeller driven aircraft that he had spent several weeks building with his older brother. These balsa wood models were lightly constructed with a framework of light wooden struts and a covering of tissued paper soaked in 'dope' ? which was not as exciting as it sounds being some sort of PVA type liquid glue that shrinks and proofed the tissue paper that was used to wrap the fuselage and wing framework of the plane. The completed model was carefully carried by my friend and his brother from the house to the park just across the road and the engine was charged by winding the propeller around some hundred or so revolutions to tension the rubber band motor. Even with my very limited knowledge and minimal recent research into this technology I could sense trouble. The fuselage was flexing and seemed under strain. The plane was thrown into the air and although it briefly flew forwards there was a ripping noise and the main body bent through ninety degrees from the strain of the overwound rubber band. It crashed to the ground where the propeller whirled frantically for at least another minute. My friend and his brother were distraught - each blaming the other for amongst other things, faulty construction, too much propeller winding and a poor launch technique but whatever the reason the plane looked to be written off. There was some disconsolate discussion over the wasted hours and money as the three of us trudged back to their house where the plane was consigned to the bin in the garden having been deemed beyond repair. My aircraft modelling days could have ended there and then but several weeks later in a model shop in town with a few weeks pocket money I was seduced by balsa wood kit of a Jet engined fighter plane, a De Havilland Sea Vixen, if I remember correctly. The clincher was that it could be fitted with a jet engine!

This device was a small metal tapered cylinder, open at one end into which a circular pellet was inserted along with gunpowder fuse to provide a form of inflammable chemical rocket propulsion. Several weeks of intricate construction followed with several mishaps and the constant battle to keep the delicate work in progress away from being slept on by the cat or 'investigated' by the inquisitive dog. Eventually it was ready to be wrapped with pieces of tissue paper and doped. I don't really know what went wrong but my wrapping seemed to put unacceptable strain on the delicate framework and I had to come to terms with the sad truth that this was not going to be airworthy. A ceremonial end was arranged in the living room fire place but ...I still had a jet engine in my possession. Egged on by a friend who'd come over for tea and to help with the some final plane construction activities we were soon found out in the garden fixing the jet propulsion pack by means of rubber bands to a cannibalised chassis of a model car. The test run was to take place on the concrete path at the top of the garden facing towards the house. The 'Jet Car' as it was now christened was placed in the centre of the path, a fuel pellet and fuse had been installed in the engine and with eager anticipation a match was lit and applied to the end of the fuse. This quickly burnt down with a pleasing flurry of sparks. Then for some seconds nothing happened. Just as we were prepared to admit defeat there was a roar and with flames shooting out of the mouth of the engine the car shot forward down the path and some forty foot later leapt over the steps and smashed into the wall of the house where the chassis engine and all four wheels split off in different directions leaving a small black sooty mark on the whitewashed wall of the house. This always proved something of a mystery to my Dad who hadn't witnessed the test flight. In conclusion this was as good as model airplanes, it's a good job the house windows were elsewhere in the wall and that test flights would need careful future planning. Research has discovered that it was not until   August 1963 that Craig Breedlove established an unofficial world land speed record of 407 mph in a rocket powered car breaking Donald Campbell's 403 mph in Bluebird CN7 a gas turbine car that drove the wheels so there was some controversy over the use of rocket power. I am sure our test run some years previously was pretty damn close to that speed, unmanned unfortunately and I don't think that I was cruel enough to install Hammy the hamster as a test pilot.

Nostalgia, coupled with EBay has meant that adults of my generation can now acquire toys that they remember from their childhood, sometimes at ambitious prices. I was please to receive on a recent birthday this splendid vintage spinning top from friends Fiona and Simon. The original box declares it to be 'The Union Jack Gyroscopic Top with Citadel. The toy for the modern boy! And capable of tricks and experiments. I wonder if Boris has one - I am sure the combination of Tricks and the Union Jack will appeal.

Food

I am sure that if you were to take a trip back in time to the years of my childhood one of the starkest contrasts between the two eras would be in the area of food. This would apply to all aspects ranging from shopping habits, food storage, the range of food available, cooking methods and dietary preferences.

Firstly in my hometown there were no supermarkets. The largest food shop was probably a Co-operative although the greatest range of fresh food was found in the newly rebuilt Swansea indoor market opened in 1961 and before that in the open market. Our groceries usually came from one of the two family grocers in the square, supplemented by fruit and veg from the greengrocers and meat from the butchers, both local. I believe fresh fish must have meant a trip to Swansea unless there was a fishmongers in Sketty, I don't remember. Convenience food was pretty limited in my early years and it was some years even before we had a fridge which only had a tiny freezer compartment. Meat and perishables were kept in a perforated metal meat safe housed in the pantry which also had some stone shelves, probably slate to provide some rudimentary cooling. Consequently, perishables were probably bought several times a week as the flexibility of freezing and microwaves was unknown technology. I recall one of my Mum's recipes which seemed exotic at the time was a corned beef and tinned tomato pie flavoured with a tin of mulligatawny soup and also containing quarters of hard boiled eggs. These must have been good standard non-perishable ingredients.

I recently tried to recreate this and I must say to my modern palate it still seemed …..well, exotic !

More exotica was soon to arrive with the advent of Vesta packet meals. These were dehydrated savoury meals and I recall that the range included Beef curry which contained dried beef with sultanas! Paella with dried chicken chunks and dried shrimps! Chow Mein with crispy and soft noodles and a sachet of soy sauce. This not only seemed exotic but quite space age and held out a future full of jet packs and holidays on the moon as promised in the Eagle comic. These 'preserved' meals must have helped with less frequent shopping but I am unaware of the pricing relative to fresh food and in any event as soon as my brother or me spotted these 'exotica' either in the shopping or pantry we were pestering to eat them which probably wasn't very helpful. The recent pandemic has seen many of us using home delivery services to a greater extent and the prevalence of web sites even for small local businesses has helped with this. Home deliveries existed in the 1950's and for our household included the daily milk delivery, newspapers, paraffin, coal deliveries, (initially by horse and cart!!) The lemonade Corona lorry was also popular although this was a weekly call and I don't think we bought it every week. The local grocer brought the order that had been dropped off as a list the same day and random callers selling household cleaning items out of suitcases were common as well as door to door encyclopaedia salesmen in those pre Wikipedia days. In the days before phone lines became common place important news was sent by telegram with the message from vague memory being constructed by pasted printed words, (like some anonymous ransom note from a Mafia film.) They were were delivered by uniformed 'telegram boys' young guys with peaked hats on small engined red motorbikes, British made BSA Bantams I believe with distinctive buzzy engines. A telegram rarely contained good news and was often the first you would hear about a family death or the hospitalisation of someone.

The most unusual travelling salesmen were what is known in South Wales as the 'Shoni onion men.' As children we were told that they had come over from France with a bicycle laden with onions to sell here and were distinctive, (apart from the bicycle laden with onions !) by wearing what we recognised as stereotypical Frenchman's costumes of a beret, work jacket and a striped shirt, (see 'Allo Allo' the last century non-pc tv series.)

Now maybe I was a suspicious child but before I had undertaken any studies in economics it didn't strike me as terribly financially viable to travel here from France with a bicycle full of onions, an item not notable, to even my limited knowledge of foodstuffs pricing, to be a high value item. It just didn't seem to add up. Was this some fiendish French plot to infiltrate the traditional British food chain with their Gallic foodstuffs. Was it a reprisal for abandoning them in 1940 by legging it at Dunkirk. I may be onto something here as the cost of travel from France was so high we didn't know anyone who went there for their holidays. My Dad had never suggested it - he was steering clear of the place after being evacuated at Dunkirk. Also he hated onions so maybe he knew more about this than he was letting on. I was never able to check out the maths as due to my father's aversion onions were rarely seen in our house, certainly not the long French strings of them.

Subsequent research that I have kindly carried out in your behalf has uncovered the following facts, some of them contradictory.

One version claims they were Breton smallholders who would band together to charter a coaster to bring their crop over the channel to dock in Swansea or Cornwall. They would spread through the area, living rough where they could, often in sheds or barns. There they would plait the onions together in strings and load as many as they could carry onto their bikes each day to start their rounds selling in the street and door to door. They would stay for around six weeks away from their families and with their Breton language being part of the Celtic family they were welcomed in the Welsh valleys and in Cornwall. The mass journeys were described as being interrupted by wartime from 1939 to 1945 and although restarting afterwards were at much lower levels of activity. I certainly remember them in the 1950's so I now imagine massed armies of them in previous decades like a pungent cycling rush hour in Amsterdam or Copenhagen. The onion strings were described as being hung up in the kitchen from a ceiling hook. Though my Dad's dislike of the vegetable ensured this didn't happen in our house.

Another writing places the story with beginnings as far back as 1828 when a Breton, Henri Olivier, sailed from Roscoff to Plymouth with a cargo of onions and after successful sales was followed by other Breton farmers suffering poverty in post-revolution France.

It is further claimed that the rapid industrialisation in Britain had led to a shortage of agricultural workers who had migrated to the mines, ironworks and factories for better paid work. As a result the imports from France were welcomed. This made these exotic onion sellers a common sight across the land but with the Celtic language link making them particularly welcome in Wales.

One description of the trade paints a different picture almost like a gang master scenario. It was said that investors would meet often in bar to put up the funds to buy the onions at the same time recruiting a company of 20 to 30 men who were hired for the season at an agreed and usually low wage but being provided with rudimentary board and lodgings,(the 'board' I suspect was primarily onion based?)

Each group was managed by a 'master' who was responsible for finding lodgings, often derelict buildings and he also was responsible for storing the onions, fixing the pricing and ordered fresh supplies of onions when necessary. The onions were transported over in sacks and were strung together by plaiting their long leaves to make the onions more attractive, An early 'artisan' marketing ploy? The onions were originally carried on long sticks with notches cut into them to hold the onion strings. The more familiar bicycle only started to be used early in the 20th century.

It was traditional for the sailings to start from Roscoff on the day after the Fete of Saint Barbe at the end of July with sailing boats in early times often being at sea for up to a week. Apart from discomfort (and presumably an overpowering aroma of onions for the voyage!) there were other more serious dangers. In 1905 the steam ship Hilda ran aground near St Malo on the french coast and 74 onion sellers drowned with only six survivors of the shipwreck, 5 of whom were onion men.

The inter-war period between 1919 and the early 1930's is thought to be the high point of the trade. Trade was interrupted by the 1939-45 war but although it resumed afterwards there were other difficulties. The UK government keen to promote home grown produce and reduce imports introduced trade tariffs and also inducements to home farmers. It is thought by 1970 the numbers coming to sell were reduced to only some 140.

The work was hard with long hours and uncomfortable living conditions with the added problem of being away from home for several months often housed in condemned houses and old warehouses in a climate colder and wetter than at home. As British farmers increasingly grew their own onions together with the rise of the supermarkets the Shoni onion men of my childhood just became a memory, but a nice one.

Despite or perhaps because of the lack of onions in our house my Mum cooked a number of recipes that proved very popular during my childhood. These were mostly non-savoury or lets be more specific - cakes and puddings! I think previous generations had a sweeter tooth although browsing down the supermarket aisles now there still seem a healthy supply of non-healthy sugar based foodstuffs. I am not saying that manufactured ranges of cakes, biscuits etc didn't exist then just that in our house, at any rate, many of the sweeter recipes were home baked. It seems ironic when the tv schedules are full of cookery programmes and baking competitions that sale of ready meals and take away sales in this country are at an all time high. It's as if cookery has become a spectator sport - that's just my view.

My Mum's culinary repertoire in the 1950's included her lemon meringue pie, a labour intensive dish that required separating egg whites and yolks, squeezing lemons and making pastry for the base. This dish as with the others was prepared in a large ceramic mixing bowl, using a hand whisk and cooked in a gas oven without a timer. It was a regular family favourite. Any baking of cakes was the opportunity to help with the washing up proceeded by scraping the residue if the cake mix or icing with a spoon as a special treat. Cakes and biscuits were cooked from scratch without mixes. Chocolate icing was made with cocoa and icing sugar and butter. Similarly lemon icing with squeezed lemons, vanilla extract for - yes, vanilla - an extract from a small bottle and rarer coffee icing as coffee in my early childhood was less common at home than tea, made with coffee from a bottle of the improbably named Camp coffee.

A large glass bowl was used for home made trifle. This was a layered construction with a foundation of jelly in the base, usually red strawberry dotted with chunks of stale cake from the previous week, if available, also pineapple chunks if my Mum was in an extravagant mood or maybe to offset the staler cake. This was followed by a first storey of blancmange , usually bright pink in colour and not my favourite ingredient. The 'roof' was a mixture of cold custard, sometimes with swirls of fresh cream and dotted with hundreds and thousands sugar sweets - the colours of which bled into the custard

I say sometimes because the shelf in the pantry where Mum kept the baking ingredients was well known to me, my brother and visiting friends and although the sweeter ingredients were often masked by a sentry line of bags of flour we were not deterred. Occasional pilfering of the glace cherries and sweet toppings provided the interim sugar rush for us young 'dentists friends' between the all too frequent visits to local sweetshops. The secret was always to leave some in the jars or packets so as not to arouse suspicions.

I was fortunate enough to have a Mum who actively encouraged sweet consumption by making homemade toffee. It wasn't her fault, in those days sugar consumption was seen as giving necessary energy to growing youngsters and adults alike. But the toffee fully embraced this idea. I believe the ingredients were sugar (of course), butter and Lyles golden syrup, (always known as treacle and from a distinctive green and gold metal tin.)

One the front of the tin was a drawing of a 'sleeping' Lion surrounded by a swarm of bees with the slogan below -"out of the strong came forth sweetness."

Now at that time I had not unreasonably concluded that the Lion, well known for bravery and fearlessness was favourably disposed towards the bees and they were existing together 'sweetly' in a harmonious relationship. My parents never dissuaded me of this with the truth that this was - shock horror

-A DEAD LION !

and the bees had nested in the corpse and were making honey there. It seemed an unlikely scenario - maybe the bees en masse had killed the lion? What is even stranger now I have researched it is that the Lyle company had registered the trademark in 1904 with the owner an Abraham Lyle who was a deeply religious man and was inspired by a bible story in the Book of Judges. It tells of Samson, the famous biblical strong man, travelling to the land of the Philistines in search of a wife. En route he killed a lion. On his return journey he saw that a swarm of bees had formed a honeycomb in the carcass.

The Wikipedia entry doesn't tell us whether he found a wife and whether she was a philistine ? I can reveal that further bible studies undertaken by me on your behalf that indeed he did. The story doesn't end happily for Samson, or the 30 people he killed over a dispute over a riddle involving the Lion and the bees when his wife, who was a Philistine, revealed the answer. He also rejected her and it seems the bees were the only winners in the whole story.

What is the most amazing thing to me now is that this story was thought to be a sound basis for an advertising slogan for a product favoured by children - well different times!

Away from the more famous holy Bible I managed to find a cut out fading page of newspaper between the pages of one of my Mum's bibles - 'Modern Cookery Illustrated. The scrap contains a recipe that I believe was my Mum's toffee recipe:-

'Two Sweets Easy to Make

Toffee - Dissolve 1 tablespoon treacle or syrup teacup boiling water and pour over 1/2 lb butter, cut up into pan with 3/4 lb sugar (brown is best). Boil for 15-20 minutes, then pour into lightly buttered tin.
Do not move until quite set.'

It omits to say do not let small children sample while still boiling hot which seemed something my Mum had to contend with or any reference to the half an hour to be spent cleaning the tray and the saucepan in the absence of a dishwasher. Still I loved it and still have the majority of my own teeth.'

As we lived in Wales it's not surprising that welsh cakes were a staple item on the menu of home baked cakes. These were made from a mixture in the white and yellow dimpled mixing bowl with the mixture sometimes enlivened by the addition of currants or sultanas. The welsh cakes themselves were cooked as a kind of drop scone on an iron hot plate heated up on top of the gas ring where they would be quickly baked on both sides. They were usually served with a sprinkling of caster sugar. I always thought the insides had a flavour similar to the uncooked cake mix scrapings that I was allowed during 'helping' sessions of baking. This was likely as the welsh cakes were probably not entirely baked within before they were removed from the hot iron. Another local delicacy, enjoyed less frequently, and with mixed enthusiasm, is laver bread, harvested from seaweed and sold in Swansea market. Difficult to accurately describe it looks rather unappetisingly like a cross between boiled spinach and a cowpat. Happily it tastes more like spinach with a salty infusion of the sea. I think it is the slightly slimy texture that puts people of but it is cited as a superfood high in iron. One recommendation is to fry it with a mixture of oatmeal and serve with your fried breakfast.

Another rather alarming discovery amongst my Mum's cook books was one that belonged to her mother and was described on the cover as "For use with the New World regulo-controlled gas cooker."
but titled Radiation Cookery Book ! Now I suppose strictly speaking heating is a form of radiation and cookery at its most elementary level is merely heating food - but really, not an encouraging title but then the date inside was 1932 so I suppose the atomic bomb was still to come.
As well as the cakes and sweet dishes my Mum did have home made savoury recipes, admittedly of varying popularity to my palate. One was a local example of a quiche recipe that my Mum called egg and bacon tart. It wasn't enlivened by onions or garlic in our house and I always thought the bacon too rubbery but was too polite to say so. There were various pies, steak and kidney as well as liver and bacon being two I remember also a similar recipe but with fish

flakes instead of meat. I was always more circumspect about this having occasionally found a fish bone. Pies topped with mashed potatoes, cottage pie, I guess were also popular with sometimes home made mince meat using a kitchen mincer clamped to the kitchen work surface to eke out leftover Sunday roasts. Sausage rolls with flakey pastry and sausage meat was another popular dish as were home made cheese straws. Sausages were also deployed in the dish Toad in the Hole, hardly an appetising label for a pleasant sausage dish baked in a Yorkshire pudding mix. Chicken was a rarity in those days before cheap 'factory birds,' and I am not sure ever tasted turkey in my childhood as I think we had chicken at Christmas but I may have been mistaken. The other ingredient that seemed much more prevalent then were jams, chutneys and pickles. Tinned fruit was enhanced by Carnation evaporated milk, sweet and creamy out of a tin. Fussels condensed milk was another tinned addition and this was much sweeter and thicker although an opened tin did not last long if it was in the fridge as a sticky spoonful was very tempting.

Television

This was a novelty in my early childhood and I have already mentioned the fire hazards, at least in our house, of the early sets. The other limitation was the range of channels on offer - namely ONE - the BBC and not even called BBC 1 because - well there was only one. I don't know when we started to watch ITV or Independent Television to give it the full title but I recall more American made content and of course, horror of horrors - Adverts !

I have discovered that the Redifusion channel, the first independent television franchise was launched in September 1955 but only in parts of the country.

Television Wales and the West TWW, had to wait until January 1958 before we could be exposed to 'I Love Lucy', Sunday Night at the London Palladium and toothpaste adverts among other cultural treats.

Also new tv aerials were necessary and older sets required adapting. I don't know if this applied to our own highly flammable model but it is clear the spread of choice was slowed by a number of barriers.

Apart from any costs of adaption there was also a certain resistance to what some saw as 'low brow; populist content particularly American imports but this seems surprising given the influence of Hollywood in the 20th Century cinema. This resistance cannot have been very strong because viewing figures published at the end of the first year had ITV programmes dominating the ratings with only two BBC shows in the top twenty, amazingly one was 'Highland Fling ' at number 14! Although I remember later shows and many were ITV ones with Robin Hood, Ivanoe (with Roger Moore 'acting' in the title role) and imported cartoons such as Deputy Dawg and Popeye my early viewing was 'Watch with Mother' which I believe was on in the afternoon at around 4 p.m.and was first screened in 1952.

There were five programmes on the five days, four of them puppet shows and I can still remember the sequence.

Monday afternoon was picture book which I think must have been educational and for helping youngsters with reading, (and probably a bit boring as I don't remember any details.)

Tuesday was Andy Pandy a somewhat wet character wearing a silly hat and a striped sort of jump suit. His sidekicks were a teddy, I think named Teddy, these were unsophisticated days in mass media - see also Hammy the Hamster - really ! But also he lived with Looby Lou an equally inept Rag Doll. I am unsure about the relationships but I think they all slept together in a large wicker basket from which they blearily emerged at the beginning of each programme. Teddy was my favourite and at an early age I envied his tolerance in

dealing with the other two. Whilst looking for an image to show you I discover that the programme has been immortalised on a stamp - Andy and Teddy without Looby Lou, thankfully.

Wednesday took the madness up several notches with Bill and Ben the Flowerpot men.Their insanity started linguistically with an inability to speak clearly with 'Flobbalob' being a favourite word, with two other characters. A weed called - yes, Weed! and a tortoise that I think was called Slowcoach but appeared to be pronounced - Flobbalob ? They episodes always ended with a song asking 'was it Bill or was it Ben that ...... insert some incident in the story. I guess

to keep the youngsters attention and develop reasoning skills though this was after suspending all known five year old logic that people could be made out of flowerpots and talk gibberish. Still we had already been exposed to Punch and Judy shows on the beach or in the park with lots of high energy mindless violence from the psychopathic Mr Punch so the gentle nonsense of the Flowerpot men must have been a relief. The flowerpot men appeared to live in terror of the gardener who was never seen but any suggestion of his arrival would have them jerkily bounced on their puppet strings back into their two large flowers pots. Presumably to avoid being cannibalised to 'pot on' any bedding plants. It was all rather surreal but entertained me in those simpler times.

Thursday was 'Rag, Tag and Bobtail,' remembered by me as a gentle pastoral woodland adventure for a Hedgehog, Mouse and Rabbit but a quick refresher on Youtube today has been quite a shock. Now given that in 1950's suburban South Wales the only hedgehogs to be seen were squashed in the road, (except for my Dad's trilby cemetery capture - see the earlier chapter on Playing.) Mice were not encouraged in our house and the last one was was bitten in half by our dog after the cat had refused to catch it. Rabbits were most commonly seen hanging up outside butchers shops and our own rabbit ownership had been short-lived.

Alarmingly the production team of Rag, Tag and Bobtail had clearly used all three of these as inspiration for their characters. This production used glove puppets and ropey ones they were too. They looked like they had been reconstructed from roadkill. Bobtail was particularly disturbing seeming to have the head of a much smaller rabbit grafted onto the bulbous torso of a large one. The storyline in the episode I recently watched on Youtube, (for the purposes of research) was a particularly improbable on involving dowsing for water with pointy sticks and a bunch of baby rabbits covered in mud. Now I don't want to disparage the 'dowsing community' maybe it's now become respectable and it's never a good idea to upset people who go about with pointy sticks - whatever their beliefs.

Although Bobtail somewhat gave the game away by announcing the ground was a bit squishy underfoot at about the same time the dowsing stick pointed down ? I can't vouch whether future episodes had the furry mammals dressed up as druids or carrying out ouija board seances but there's plenty of material like that to employ.

Friday ended the week on a more realistic (?) note with the WOODENTOPS, an everyday story of a wooden puppet family and their spotty dog. My research tells me that only 26 episodes were made so they must have been an early example of the staple of BBC programming - the Repeat ! If only they had spoken to the script writers of Rag, Tag and Bobtail I'm sure they could have extended the series using more improbable storylines. The episode I watched for the purposes of research wasn't an epic storyline and was mostly about Baby Woodentop throwing his blanket out of his pram, several times.

The family looks to be the standard mid- century nuclear family on which later classic such as the Simpsons call on for inspiration.

There is Mummy and Daddy Woodentop, The twins, Jenny and Willy, Baby Woodentop and Spotty dog. Mr and Mrs Scrubbit are embryonic Ned Flanders and there is Buttercup the cow. The episode I have watched for research was so mind numbingly boring that I am not sure I can find out any more - at least not until I have exhausted the entire Flowerpot Men back catalogue that is vastly superior in invention and dialogue.

My favourite character Spotty dog appears and tramples the flower bed in a four wooden leg way and shows a distinct aversion to the idea of a bath but an impressive mastery of the english language both in understanding but also in a canine vocalisation. The other surprise is that a song or more of a chant really that I remember from my childhood - the iconic :-

"What are we having for dinner today ?
Sawdust and Hay for dinner today !"
had its origin in this very episode. Still on the whole of all the five programmes I am favouring Bill and Ben as the top choice- it has legs, albeit ones made of flowerpots.

Other contemporary programmes were probably as creaky - I remember some of their names without actually recalling many details. Early ones were Mr Pastry, a clown, Billy Bean and his funny machine (?), Muffin the Mule (???), Bengo the puppy and of course Sooty and Sweep.

Music was another world as Radio One and the pirate radio stations were not to arrive until well into the next decade - the mid 1960's which was a whole new world. Music exposure was mostly via the Light programme (later to become Radio 2.) So my musical education came via Forces favourites and Uncle Mac on Saturday mornings. Most of the memorable records, to me at least, were the comedy records - The Three Billy Goats Gruff, Sparkie's magic piano (later to be ripped off by Cher among others!) Bernard Cribbens, Hole in the ground, Lonnie Donegan's 'My Old Man's a Dustman,' Tommy Steel's Little White Bull, Max Bygrave's Toothbrush song as well as songs from the musicals. Other gems of the era included the Chipmunks -high pitched cover songs and 'The Runaway Train' and the 'Big Rock Candy Mountain?' which contained the improbable lines of 'the Cigarette trees and lemonade springs and cops with wooden legs and bulldogs with rubber teeth'. The song was written in the

1920's but the radio played a later version by Burl Ives - weird stuff.

Pop music from Elvis, Cliff and the Shadows etc were still in the future for me. It's interesting that the comedy records maybe prepared my generation for 'our pop music' to come later. An interesting fact is that Adam Faith one of the early successes, copying Buddy Holly's hiccuping vocal style was the first number record for the Parlophone record label and was their only pop act having previously concentrating on comedy records. Of course the label was to experience much more success a few years later with some little known outfit of scousers produced by George Martin. Years later whilst elbowing my way to the bar in a theatre interval I was aware of pushing past a small blonde man to get to the bar before the second act. As I turned to apologise I recognised him as Adam Faith - it is to my eternal credit that I resisted saying to him "What Do Ya Want?"

Of course it is easy to forget now that TV, the magical, post war entertainment for the masses existed in shades of grey on temperamental, small dim screens and was only transmitted for a limited number of hours a day. But it was through this medium along with occasional glimpse of Pathe News at the cinema that we were exposed to views of the world beyond our home town. It would be hard to believe as a child seeing world famous sights such as the University Boat race, Trooping the Colour, the House of Parliament, St Peter's Square or the Eiffel Tower, the White Cliffs of Dover, the Derby or Chelsea Flower show all of which as adults many of us have experienced first hand; these seem far off visions brought only via the tv screen.

Mentioning the White Cliffs of Dover reminds me of an appropriate 'white lie' I once found myself telling. I was taking a small party of American visitors from our US company owners from our Surrey office back to Brighton after a tedious day of meetings when one of them asked me whether the white cliffs of Dover were really white and how far away they were from where we were. A short detour to Rottingdean allowed them to get out and take photos of the Sussex Severn Sister cliffs which, not wishing to spoil their joy, I assured them were the famous white cliffs of Dover.

The next day I had to swear colleagues in the office to secrecy so that for that day the Dover cliffs could be easily glimpsed from Brighton. The visitors were pleased and maybe honesty isn't always the best policy.

The Sea

I realise that I have spent most of my life within the sight of the sea either living on the coast or with a body of water within stone throwing distance. This sequence includes my childhood homes where Swansea bay was visible from my bedroom window.

Swansea Bay viewed from Tycoch.

At University in Aberystwyth there was a sea view, this time of Cardigan Bay. Working in the south east of England, living in Kent and Sussex but with office window views of the English Channel.
I briefly rented a flat during my first year of full time work after university, a stone's throw from the beach at Sandgate in South Kent.

There was a short period working and living in Surrey which I was pleased to move away from and have always wondered whether their absence of sea air has stifled the personalities

of people there, at least some of them that I knew. Recently moving back to Wales my home overlooks a quayside and a dock with a sandy beach a ten minute walk away. Our holiday home is a short walk from the sea and we have sea views in both our homes. Even when living in Surrey my house had a small pond and when living in the Sussex High Weald we spent a not inconsiderate sum of money and effort to create a garden pond large enough to put a small boat on and go fishing from. So water and the sea was an important part of my childhood and has remained so ever since.

Where I live now, next to one of Swansea's oldest docks was during my childhood a destination with my Dad on some Sunday mornings when it was possible for the public to go on board ships that were docked. It was particularly interesting if they were naval vessels and I know my Dad would be surprised to find me living in a quayside development near the site of those boyhood visits. Looking through a box of old 35 mm slides recently I found one taken with my first 35 mm camera around the age of ten or eleven, it was a photo of a row of large dockside cranes, two remaining ones are visible to me now out of my study's window.

The two photos are shown above.

Visits to the beach were frequent in my childhood. From our house it would be a walk of a little over half an hour through Singleton park to cross the Mumbles road onto the large sandy expanse of the bay. As an adult I found most of the beaches near my home in the south of England to be singularly linear, narrow and usually stony or pebbles with patches of gritty sand. Very different to the sandy beaches of my youth in Swansea and Gower.

The earliest memories of Swansea beach would be of a regular walk from our house in Tycoch down to the beach through Singleton park then along the seashore to cut up to the Strand before the river Tawe. This would take place in the afternoon with my brother in a push chair and the objective was to meet my Dad from work. He worked in the offices of Unit Superheaters, a large factory off the Strand on the banks of the river. I can remember seeing the hordes of workers coming out of the gates with me looking to spot my Dad before we walked up to the High Street to catch a bus home. This being a distance of some four miles I can only think it was an occasional walk and punctuated with several stops, hopefully for a drink or an ice cream as it wasn't the norm in those days to go everywhere clutching bottles of drink.

Before we had a family car a trip to Caswell, one of our favourite bays in Gower was a bus ride away. A glorious sandy beach with the bonus of rock pools to explore but the main occupation as children after a splash about in the normal freezing waters of the Bristol Channel was the building of sandcastles. This was best attempted when the tide was incoming and there was a race to construct a moat and fortress walls which we would sit behind until the waters inevitably breached the walls and wetness was added to the discomfort already caused by the sand - easily endured when you are five or six years old. Caswell bay or more correctly the cliffs there, (composed of oolitic limestone - if I remember correctly) were the site of different activities during one of my years at Bishop Gore Grammar school. It was decreed that those of us studying a majority of arts courses for GCE's should have some additional 'science' studies. So for some two lessons a week some two dozen of the 'artistic temperament' had Geology lessons. This was taught by an enthusiastic Science master who I remember we called Benjie so I guess he was a Mr or Dr Benjamin. His enthusiasm extended to taking a coach load of us one morning to the cliffs at Caswell all armed with hammers and chisels brought from our father's sheds. I don't remember any injuries or hospitalisations so his confidence in our fossil hunting skills appears not to have been misplaced.

If any of the current teaching profession or parents from a different generation are reading this I can just see you imagining the difficulty in completing a credible Risk Assessment document to allow such an expedition in the 21st century. I repeat the mantra - these were different times! The trip was memorable and we came back with fossils and I am sure to the relief of the dictatorial organisation (known as the National Trust.) I have seen that there are still plenty of fossils there today.

The public parks that my home town is still blessed with were also a source of water based activities. There must be some primeval memory of the human species emerging from water that periodically draws us back and this seems particularly true of small children. The local parks were a destination in spring time to collect frogspawn or tadpoles to take home and watch them develop their legs. I don't really remember what happened then until in later years we had a small garden pond that could act as a nursery for the froglets the would hide in the adjacent rockery and make my Mum jump when she was weeding. A few of the parks had boats for hire for awkward rowing half hours and Brynmill park had a small part of the pond for toy sailing boats and a motor boat that took passengers on a trip around the large lake much to the annoyance of the duck population. Local streams were available for games of 'Pooh sticks' though we didn't call it that. Later in my early teens along with many boys at that time I developed a keen enthusiasm for fishing, in ponds, streams and lakes as well as the sea but this was all in the future.

Church

Religion played a larger part in the lives of the majority of people in post war Britain and specifically for my family it was the Church of England in Wales. Yes, although in line with the popular conception of Wales being a nation of chapel goers and the abundance of chapel buildings large and small throughout the principality, C of E churches are also common and at the time were regularly attended by large congregations. Religion was a regular part of our lives from prayers in school to regular attendance at church and Sunday school and with it being a day of religious observance shops and most businesses were closed to allow religious attendances. Television schedules were even shorter than usual and these and radio programmes took on a more sober nature and were often religious in their content. Cubs and Scouts also used prayer and took part in church parades. Religious instruction was part of the regular school curriculum and the bible stories were well known to virtually all children.

The local church in Tycoch, All Souls was very much an integral part of the local community. The church was built in the mid 1950's and completed and consecrated when I was six in 1957. The church hall nearby was built some three years later, partially assisted by parishioner workgroups. I remember my Dad and other members of the congregation digging some of the foundations. Once built it was useful for fetes and group meetings adding to the social life of Tycoch. We were told in school that Ty Coch was welsh for Red House that previously existed but I have also read that it could be Tir Coch, meaning red land, so you take your choice but until I left school for university it was where I did my growing up. In our family fairly regular attendance would include the morning communion service complete with a sermon from the vicar. Sunday school attendees stayed after the service and be joined by other pupils who hadn't had the luxury of the previous hour or so's indoctrination and would be taken to the back while the communion took place and then Sunday School began. Attendance whilst not universal but very common so much so that a friend told me that as a child she believed attendance was a legal requirement for all children like day school. The cynical might suggest this was a rumour encouraged by parents to get an hour to read the sunday papers before the return of their charges. Sounds plausible to me ! I remember a few bible stories and hymns from those hours. I also remember some boys enlivening proceedings by producing a slow worm or pet mouse from their best blazer pocket perhaps secure that retribution would be more 'christian' rather than the wrath of god unleashed by such behaviour from teachers and heads in day school.

Society in my part of South Wales was much more of a monoglot culture than today and the world of Islam or Buddism or indeed any other of the great religions of the world would have been outside our youthful experience. Indeed in the C of E schools pupils of other faiths were excused the religious part of school assemblies and bizarrely invited in to hear school announcement, usually about sports team results or the more alarming 'summons of miscreants' to see the Head afterwards in his study.

In my early teens, along with many contemporaries, I attended confirmation classes for several months which added another commitment to a Sunday. I can only think that at that tender age we were more biddable to undertake such initiatives. Looking back I struggle to believe that for a short time again in my early teens I performed the duties of an altar server along with school-friends Roger and Dennis. Even after the long time gap I feel embarrassed to remember it. I can only think that the humiliation of wearing a long red gown and white starched surplice (which I believe had some kind of frilly collar !) was only palatable as an alternative to joining the choir, for which I definitely didn't possess the necessary skills for. The only upside I remember was taking it in turns to tunelessly ring the single church bell for ten minutes before the service began. I liked to think the tuneless 'gonging' row going out across the community's houses not long after nine a.m. on Sunday morning may have irritated some of my teachers or other folk within earshot that had annoyed me.

Differences

If we were to find ourselves back in the years of my childhood, what would be the parts of life then that would strike us as so different and in some cases shock us as commonplace then but bordering on the bizarre to modern eyes? In no particular order or priority of significance I make a few observations drawing on my distant memories of those times.
A major difference then was smoking. The majority of adult men and many women smoked and the commonplaceness of this meant that all the accoutrements of the habit littered homes, offices a and forms of transport. Apart from the danger of fire, which I have mentioned elsewhere here, there must have been the smell that accompanied this on clothes and compounded by full ashtrays and lingering tobacco fumes. This could often be increased by the presence of a pipe smoker who seemed to up the unpleasantness several notches. One of my grandfathers and another uncle were dedicated pipe men and no doubt their pungency dominated many a family gathering. This was also in the days before the popularity of fresh air sprays, scented candles or even extractor fans.I guess we were immune to it as it was normality.
I was struck by the absurdity of this in recent times some ten years ago when I needed to attend a medical appointment at a doctor's surgery in Crete and before he examined me, in this case for possible concussion, he put his cigarette, still burning in an ash tray on his desk. Also his advice was to avoid strong alcohol for a few days but social drinking and smoking should be ok ! I did explain to him that I wasn't about to compound my health worries by embracing the hazardous habit at my advanced age.

Another strong contrast would be the lack of traffic on the streets and the rarity of family car ownership together with the sense of anticipation as to whether the car would actually start ! Every journey must have been much more of an adventure. The novelty of family car ownership brought

about the new concept of 'going out for a drive.' This meant the family would get in the car on, say a Sunday afternoon, and set off with no real destination in mind giving the whole expedition a sense of randomness and also a devil may care atmosphere. The relative emptiness of the roads must have helped with this and to my mind this contrasts so much with today where even in retirement we will book for a meal somewhere even for a mid week lunch, put the destination into the phone app or sat nav and have an element of planned itinerary that was not so normal then.
Communication was basically by letter or telephone, in many households by using the red phone box at the end of the road.

Entertainment was relatively restricted with television on short hours and limited initially to one channel. Cinema was more popular than today and children had their own Saturday morning cinema clubs. In our case this was in the local Odeon in Sketty where for 6 old pence you could enjoy a whole morning of films, or 9 pence to sit in the balcony where you wouldn't be targeted by rowdier kids dropping sweets or their wrappers on you. It was a dilemma whether the extra thrupence spent would deprive you of an amount of your own fresh sweets against the likelihood of a projected and possibly pre-sucked sticky one landing on your head.
The entertainment was formulaic with some cartoons, a series film - probably a cowboy or detective theme, then a longer film again maybe western or pirate themed. I must confess I can't remember any of them but like other childhood events it was a step on the road to later adult freedoms. My parents also were cinema fans although the arrival of two children must have restricted their attendances. I do remember being taken by them to see some Walt Disney films, also 'Genevieve,' a comedy film about the London to Brighton vintage car run. We watched the film again recently and it surprised me that it was in brilliant colour. When we watched the first time it both my Mum and me would have been amazed that we would enjoy the run some forty plus years later in my 1966 Volkswagen

camper van. My Mum was surprised that there were so many Volkswagens and no early vintage cars. She wasn't aware that almost every weekend there's a car run for specific models such as Minis, Jaguar's and even Smart cars.
The Genevieve film also starred Kenneth More who seemed popular in the 1950;s also starring as RAF's Douglas Bader in 'Reach for the Sky', which i was taken to see. Around the same time my Dad took me to see the real Douglas Bader who was re-opening Swansea's Fairwood Airport. At the time Douglas Bader was seen by the public as a real life hero attracting the attention reserved today for 'hero' celebrities such as Tom Cruise.
On an associated train of thought, part of Fairwood Airport was used some ten years later by teenage children and their parents for ad-hoc driving lessons before the youngsters were considered to be ready for instruction on actual roads. The wide disused runways were excellent for practising steering and clutch control. I don't know if any of those Sunday morning practices resulted in uninsured collisions between 16 or 17 year olds in their parents' cars, at least I didn't cause or see any!

Clothing was another difference. Apart from the predominance of heavy traditional material such as woollen jumpers, thick cotton shirts and flannel trousers there was the lack of logos and let's be blunt - fashion. Every boy was dressed in the style that prince Charles has embraced for his entire life. Some of the preference for woollens was because of the lack of central heating and the need to keep warm at bus stops etc. In part it was also because manufacturing of man made fibres hadn't progressed to the stage of the 21st century with micro fabrics, lightweight fleeces etc. Although there was a period in the 1990's when the popularity of 'shell suits' had me believe the population would soon be echoing Captain James T Kirk and the crew of the Starship Enterprise, at least sartorially. Happily this has not happened and recent fears about microfibres polluting the ocean may take us back down the woolly jumper route - we shall see.
The lack of cheap clothing imports also meant that everybody's wardrobes were smaller as the people

themselves were! This also led to expertise in mending, darning, home knitting - even unravelling old pullovers to reknit them - these were more frugal times for most folk. Also the passing down of clothes in families and from friends was much more common so that a trip to town for new clothes was a joyous experience. I was the elder brother so probably got more than my fair share of new clothes but was fortunate (or unfortunate depending on your perspective) to have an older male cousin in the next town. Fortunately after a few years I outgrew him or became more muscular or less svelte depending again on your perspective so clothing inheritance was off the agenda from him. Fashion before the teenage years was limited and probably all young boys, at least in my school, were dressed similarly. Kudos was occasionally provided by a 'snake' belt - a striped elasticated belt with an S shaped snake clasp which was popular in the 50's. I proudly wore sock garters from my cub uniform whenever possible and favoured 'Ladybird' brand T shirts because there was a coloured ladybird logo embroidered on the inside label, so maybe I had embraced more fashion snobbery than I remember. Miniature suits with short trousers or blazers were the prescribed clothes for church or Sunday school and even for visiting relatives particularly if it was a Sunday ! Making such clothes a ready target for cream or trifle spillages - not terribly sensible really but it was the times.

Clothes were mostly bought from department stores in town and I remember Lewis Lewis, David Evans and C and A but I guess there were others. Boutiques were several years away in the mid 1960's. I also have a recollection of a mail order catalogue - Marshall Ward I think, and I guess the items came through the post and if they didn't fit - well you would grow into it or if too small then there was always my younger brother. Credit cards had not been invented so most purchases must have been in cash but I am sure shoe expenses for two growing boys, who mainly walked everywhere, were a constant worry. A local shoe shop had innovated a 'shoe club' where customers made regular weekly payments into an account and shoes could be bought against the balance when needed. I guess this was the start of a slippery slope towards the credit mountain in the economy at present but it must have been a help at the time. On the subject of cash in shops this was the era of other innovations or at least it seemed so to a young boy. One shop had a vacuum tube system with took your cash and a sale note in a small metal canister which was then fired through a tube system transported by magic although I now know it was compressed air, to later return with your receipt and any change from somewhere in the bowels of the shop. An alternative was some wire catenary system that achieved the same effect by shooting the projectiles along wires. I guess like the Daleks, the drawback of the second system was the inability to go upstairs. Still it was fascinating to observe both systems. I guess the first was the inspiration for Elon Musk's Hyperloop although he never mentions it. To small children who were avid readers of Dan Dare these systems were certain proof that rapid transit monorail systems and the like would soon be coming to a town near you. As it was we had to make do with the

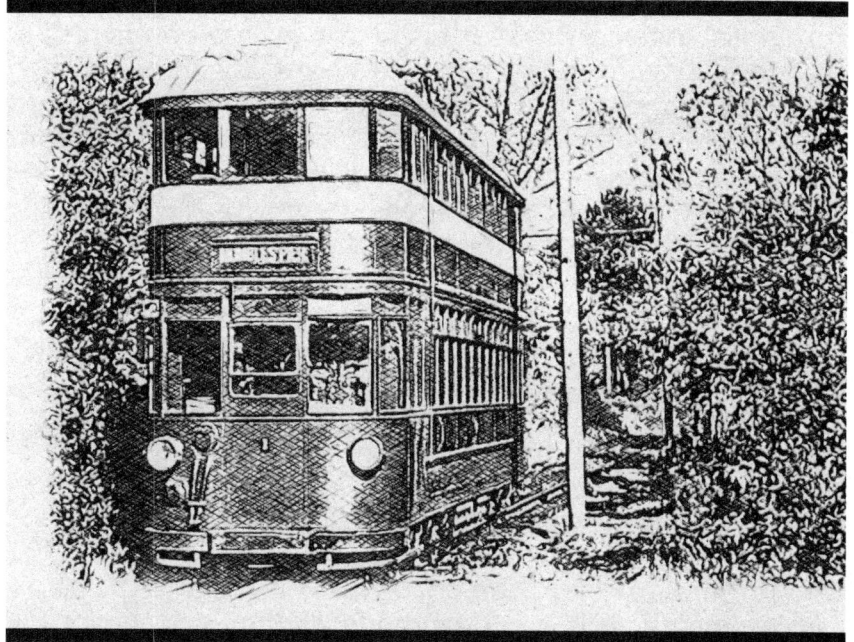

aforementioned trip on the London Underground and some rather rickety trolley buses that still existed in Cardiff. The claim to fame for our town of Swansea was the Mumbles train reputedly the oldest continuous running fare paying train system in the world - really!

My research department tells me that it was originally built under an Act of Parliament of 1804 to move limestone from the quarries of Mumbles to the mouth of the river Tawe in Swansea on tracks and initially drawn by horses. An agreement effective from 25 March 1807 allowed the carriage of fare paying passengers and it was this that made it the oldest passenger railway in the world. Steam power replaced the horses in 1877 with electrification introduced in 1928 using overhead tram lines.
The tram style trains carried 106 passengers and were often coupled as a pair giving a total carrying capacity of 212.
One of the clever things, at least to a six year old, was the way the trains didn't turn around to return to Swansea. In reality at the end of the track towards Mumbles Pier there wasn't enough room between the beach and the cliffs for a turntable. Instead the seat backs cleverly swung across so that the seats faced the opposite way. I was very impressed with this and while travelling backwards on subsequent train journeys have always regretted that this innovation hadn't been more widely adopted. Perhaps it's time will come in the era of self-driving cars which we are promised will provide a 'more lounge-like experience' - I may just submit a patent application before it's too late. So my memories were that it was an exciting way to travel around the Bay and also it must have added drama to getting across the line to the beach itself. I recall there was a bridge over the 'Slip' access point which was at the bottom of Singleton park and our normal way over to the beach. But I believe it was possible to cross the lines in other places.

The Mumbles train ran for the last time on the morning of the 5th January 1960 and its demise has been regretted by many ever since. It had been bought two years earlier by South Wales Transport , a bus company and was a victim of the rise of the car as the preferred mode of transport. Again the route is now regularly used by thousands of cyclists and walkers and is part of the Coastal Path of Wales.

I also have an accusation to make for my generation and that is one of selfishness and by this I mean the quest to reform many aspects of the world to suit ourselves perhaps the first time in history that social mores were shaped by one generation - in this case the post war 'baby boomers', a group which by my age I am part of. Some of human progress would be part of a natural progression of improvements but other aspects seem a very real reflection of the spirit of teenage rebellion by the first generation to have a distinct teenage culture and a generation who have proved reluctant to relinquish those newly won freedoms. Let me provide some examples.

Clothes

The 1950s and the 1960's saw for the first time whole generations who no longer dressed the same way as the previous generation. There may have been different 'tribes' from the Teds, Mods, Skinheads, Hippies and Goths but what they had in common was they did not dress like their parents.

But perversely subsequent generations have broadly reverted to uniformity so that you can see families of three generations wearing 'identical uniforms' be it logo T shirts, baseball hats, trainers and cargo shorts or trousers. Other families can be dressed alike in Boden clothes or similar brands ready for the yacht club but apart from greying hair and middle age spread generations are mirroring one another. There is also the trend for mothers and daughters to still shop together and say -"Yes my daughter is my best friend.." - the desperate clinging to youth - we are all at it - the pain of skinny jeans on not so skinny legs.

The other major changes include the lack of formal dress in the workplace. When I started my first job after university, as another anachronism, the Graduate Trainee. Here you would start at an inflated salary because of your perceived potential and superior abilities and be moved through the various departments of a large organisation being shown the

various duties therein - 'having a go' yourself before being swiftly being moved on before the workers could find out your true abilities and more worryingly what you were being paid to 'half do' their job and try to assassinate you! All the time this was performed in the early 1970's in a three piece suit, shirt and tie, possibly cuff- links with beard and shoulder length hair closely resembling the defendants in court at some major drugs bust having been told by their barrister to look smart for the judge, (this despite the fact that judges wear
a wig and appear to be in a borrowed father xmas suit.).

Eating out and In
In the 1950's for people outside the Bertie Wooster class it would be unusual to regularly 'eat out.' Perhaps for a special occasion such as a birthday or anniversary but in any event people from that time would be amazed at the range and quantity of opportunities for eating away from home. Yes there were restaurants and dining rooms in hotels as well as some fish and chip cafes but going to them would be for special treats and holidays. The other change was the whole entertaining at home. Although my parents could be described as being of the new professional class, if you wanted to find a label, I can't recall any dinner parties. There were children's parties and relatives would invite us or come around to us for tea. This would normally be sandwiches and perhaps tinned fruit and cream or maybe trifles.

Being Spontaneous
In some ways there may have been more spontaneity given that instant communication was not universal as it is today and the majority of households in the 1950's did not even have a land-line phone. So visits could and often were more random although there was a counter to this in that some events would follow a regular routine to avoid the element of surprise so that catering or even being at home was predicted. My Mum always carried a small pen and a notepad in her hand back to leave the required 'we called but you were out' message. At least it seemed they were out, maybe they didn't want two lively young boys in their house or they

had heard about the non-musical' performances at my grannnie's house in Hanover Street. They may even have personal experience if they lived in the neighbourhood. Routines such as the regular Sunday afternoon visit by or to the grandparents became rituals. Happening at the same times on the same day of the week which must have helped with any catering demands before the days of freezer ownership and shops closed on sundays. I am sure that children of the fifties would have resented the tight apron strings applied to today's youngsters by their parents as with the lack of communications meant that arriving home late from school or delayed from an outing to a friends house couldn't always be a cause for concern. Often the answer was 'I didn't realise what the time was - sorry,' was all that was required.

Music
Radios and TV's were common in homes in post war Britain but with differences. There was usually only one television in the house and watched less frequently because of limitations of both channels and schedules. Radios or 'Wireless' as it was called was initially anything but, as they were normally plugged inti the mains, bulky and required a warm up time for the valves. I remember being very pleased to have a second set at home which was on my bedside table and wired into the light socket in the ceiling by means of an adaptor. Listening was allowed for a half an hour at bedtime for such gems as the Clitheroe Kid and the Goon show, (both shamelessly recycled on BBC radio today and pretty creaky.) The advent of portable battery radios seemed a breakthrough thought the first one the family had required a large expensive battery that seemed to expire prematurely and the radio, Ekco I believe, weighed a ton. Around the time of my tenth or eleventh birthday transistor radios became available and I remember one Christmas were I asked for one as did many of my school friends so we were able to inflict tinny sounding broadcasts on the public whilst out and about, often while listening to different stations. I clearly remember details of mine, it was black plastic with a leather case and a silver chrome grill over the speaker.

Buttons to change the band wave from medium to long wave, fm not yet available, at least on my radio, and numbers showing the position on the tuning band appearing through a little perspex window.

The range of stations was relatively limited with the BBC yet to launch Radio 1 and the pirate radio stations to only sail over the horizon in a few years time. Radio Luxembourg was transmitting with the unreliable signal stronger at night so that pop music could be listened to under the bedclothes through the small earpiece that came with the radios. As well as music there was US style commercial sponsorship with the legendary advert for Horace Batchelor and his iffy sounding 'Infra-Draw Method' for increasing your chances of winning the football pools. I never understood what the scheme was or whether it worked but he was famous and memorable for spelling out of his address where you would send your money, (the last time you would probably see it!) His advert was particularly instructive on where you were to send the money to his address in Keynsham, "that's K-E-Y-N-S-H-A-M, Bristol"

My brief research tells me he was a keen watercolour artist and after his death in 1977 his estate was worth £150,000 - alright but, if his scheme was foolproof I would have expected more - but at least he made for many the name of the Keynsham and how to spell it unforgettable.

I recommend the track 'You done my brain in' on the album Keynsham by the wonderful and gloriously named Bonzo Dog Doo-Dah Band that briefly samples Mr Batchelor's sale pitch. There are many other gems on the album for readers with a keen sense of humour.

It wasn't until the early 1960's that the family acquired what is known as a 45 rpm record player powered by electricity (!), together with any music that I wanted to listen to.

Prior to this the family record player had been a wind up 78 player and hard acetate records of music for my parents. I don't recall the details of the music, maybe Bing Crosby and Pearl Carr and Teddy Johnston (?) The player itself was of the type glorified by Nipper the dog and His Master's Voice advert. Looking now at the picture I realise their set was marginally more modern but the principal was the same with

hard wire needles, kept in a small metal 'reservoir' in the base of the case and incidentally also useful as deadly shells

in our toy soldier's cannons which was a bonus and something of a mystery to my Dad who found them

embedded in sofa cushions etc after a battle that he fortunately wasn't witness to.

I believe our model was more like the one here and it was principally used by children to race cars on or project toy soldiers off the spinning turntable.

The electric Dansette was a step forward as a joint Christmas present as well as choosing a small collection of 45 singles. From memory the selected treasures included Elvis Presley's 'Return to Sender,'

Joe Brown's 'Picture of You,' The Shadows 'Wonderful Land,' 'Sun Arise' by Rolf Harris !!! (We didn't know..) The Tornadoes 'Telstar,' and Helen Shapiro's 'Walking Back to Happiness,' and 'Speedy Gonzales.' The other classics - I think there were ten or twelve in total, are lost in time, maybe a Bernard Cribbens comedy record or a Tommy Steele classic?

I believe the record player resembled the one below, I know it was blue and certainly similar.

Names

Formality also continued with the use of names.

This was a time before the instant use of first names. Neighbours and local shopkeepers were known by their surnames even if they lived next door and had been known for years. Friends may eventually graduate to the uncle or aunt prefix leading to confusion over family trees.

Houses

From the perspective of a 1950's childhood the homes of today would seem extravagant and unrecognisable from the simpler home comforts of that time. The first house I remember from the age of three had an outside toilet and the only running water was in the kitchen. A few years later my Dad and uncle installed a bathroom with a sink and a bath upstairs and brought the outside toilet 'in-doors' by linking it to the kitchen by a lean to  conservatory and I seem to remember a sliding door. Very Barry Bucknell for those who remember 1950's television DIY programmes. Power points were limited to one or at most two in each room and not always that as I remember an adaptor coming down from the ceiling light in my bedroom for the mains radio - wireless it wasn't ! Central heating seem to be limited to schools and public buildings so home heating was a mixture of coal and gas fires, solid fuel ranges , electric fires - radiant or convector and dreadfully smelly paraffin heaters. Homes were warm in places but in the winter it was not unknown to wake up to frost on the inside of your bedroom window which was of course single glazed and likely to be a draughty and a loose fitting sash window that would be rattled by the buses passing by. Carpeting was not universal and often a large square in the centre of the room, or a runner up the centre of a staircase, both economy measures. Lighting must have been dimmer and limited in range compared to today although table and standard lights were popular to supplement the central ceiling rose. Embryonic home insulation measures were definitely 'low- tech' including thick door curtains and fabric 'sausages' laid across the bottom of doors as draught excluders.

This was also supplemented by patent rolls of adhesive backed foam strip that was enthusiastically stuck up around doors and window openings, reducing some of the draught whilst providing a magnet for dust, stray hairs and spiders. If a phone was in the house the phone point was usually in the hall located near the draughty front door possibly a tactic to limit the time spent on the phone. Domestic phone lines were often 'party lines' shared so that you would pick up the receiver to make a call and be able to eavesdrop on the conversation of the neighbour who shared your line although they would be alerted by a click and often a more echoey character to the call. Although this now seem bizarre I am amazed the details of phone conversations you hear today with people speaking loudly to their psychiatrist, therapist, bank, or friends discussing all sorts of personal matters - fascinating often - have people no shame?

There was also the concept of the 'front room' or best room at least there was in our house. This was a room infrequently used by the family, at least when I was younger, the television or any entertainment was in the living room in our house, which was the middle room next to the kitchen. This room had a couple of easy chairs and a small sofa as well as a dining table and four chairs with a large radio and the tv on the sideboard. Glass fronted cupboards in alcoves either side of the fireplace were used for storage of crockery and glasses etc. I remember visits to the front room in my Nana's house, my father's mother when we had a magic lantern show in the front room with the curtains drawn and glass coloured slides showing, I think, of places in Britain. Another memory of that room was when my brother and myself were sent to play in there while my grandparents and my Mum and Dad talked in the living room two rooms away. We amused ourselves playing musical duets on the piano and harmonium there, unencumbered by musical training.

Until my Dad dragged us out complaining about the blooming row that was drowning out their conversation. The kitchen in the house was a much simpler affair with fewer cupboards as shopping was a more frequent activity. I remember a metal meat safe in the larder cupboard before we acquired a small fridge with a tiny ice box so that ice cubes were an option but there wasn't enough space for frozen food.The cooker was a simple gas cooker which was also used for toast under the gas grill. The only other large appliance I recalled was a washing machine that was filled up from the tap and had a fold out wringer on top but no spin dryer. At some later stage we must have upgraded to a twin tub machine which drain into the sink. It all must have been pretty labour intensive for the housewife as in those days it was the housewife that was responsible for most domestic chores. Cleaning included beating rugs on the line although we did have a vacuum cleaner. I can only conclude it wasn't so efficient that some extra assistance was required. This was hardly surprising given coal fires, people smoking as well as the debris from two boys and a cat and a dog. Houses had additions of dado rails, picture rails as well as a fireplace in most rooms including bedrooms, the Victorians and Edwardians were big on fireplaces. All of these must have been real dust traps making household cleaning even more of a chore than it was already.

Children's bedrooms, certainly in winter, didn't double up as playrooms as it was usually only the downstairs rooms that were heated although portable electric heaters could be used for a short time to take the chill of a room before bed time but more usually it was hot water bottle taken to bed and thick feather eider downs placed on top of the sheet and blankets that would provide bedroom warmth. The intermittent use of everything was a feature of post war life. Electricity use was deemed expensive - 'Put out the lights when you leave the room', only heat rooms that are occupied, switch on water heater when required. Phone calls, once the phone arrived, were to be kept short - the profligate use of all services and centrally heated houses with all the rooms and hallways and stairs warmed and the availability of constant hot water would I am sure been regarded with disbelief and the concept of patio heaters would have been more of a shock.

As I have mentioned before, photos from the 1950's were a relative rarity compared to today with the ubiquitous camera phone. Often they only existed from special occasions such as a wedding, birthday or some other family gathering. The new arrival of a baby or pet may also have been recorded. The photo below shows me standing in the front garden of our house in Tycoch Road - quite why, I don't know and the low definition makes it difficult to date but I suspect it was the mid to late 1950's. The house is still there today although the road seems more crowded with cars parked along it. The school next door but one has been demolished and replaced by a development of flats plus a cafe on the site of one of the playgrounds. They have even removed the railings that my brother got his head stuck in but that's probably just as well.

During the early years of my secondary school we moved two roads away up the hill in Tycoch to a bungalow in Lon Bedwen and I discovered that is still there but the large garden had enough space to build another house in it. This must have reduced the burden of what was one of my regular chores, to cut the long privet hedge that bordered the plot, using hand shears, quite an onerous task for a reluctant young teenager but it got me out of the house!

Swansea

Why is Swansea here? Many settlements were historically located at the mouth of a river or on the banks of one at this is likely to be the original reason. These areas could be defended and the river mouth provided a natural harbour side for sea trade. Legend has it that the place name is derived from 'Sweyn's Ey' a Viking name - who knows, it's a nice story.
The name of the town in Welsh: Abertawe makes more sense, translated as 'mouth of the Tawe.'
A young six year old friend on his first visit saw a swan swimming on the river and the sea in the distance and said 'Swan; Sea.' So thanks Isaac, that's a good explanation for me.
Much of the medieval centre of the city was destroyed by bombing in the Second World War. There are castles and some medieval farmhouses outside the city but in any event in 1801 the town's population was estimated at a mere 6000. How did it grow to be considered as a contender for the capital of Wales, (Cardiff was declared the nation's capital as recent as 1955 but had been smaller than Swansea and Merthyr Tydfil for part of the 19th century.)
It was all down to minerals. Coal exports supported Cardiff's growth to predominance as it had for Merthyr before it and Swansea's growth was down to metallurgy too. Specifically, copper smelting with production in the lower Swansea valley reaching it's peak in the early 19th century when it's claimed that over 60 % of the world's copper was produced in the valley and exported from the port. The bizarre fact is that Swansea had no real deposits of copper ore but the juxtaposition of a number of elements combined to create this industry.
Firstly, there were abundant supplies of coal nearby.
Secondly, a canal system in the Swansea valley gave easy transport for the coal.
Thirdly, the river and later the port allowed copper ore to be imported by sea.
Fourthly, there was a legacy in the area of metal smelting expertise.

Finally, some enterprising entrepreneurs identified the opportunities of these elements to take cheap land sites for the works, encourage labour into the area from rural Wales and further afield and together build an industry of global significance at that time. The imports of copper ore deposits previously coming in relatively small quantities from mines in North Wales and Cornwall were now extended across the globe to reach out to Spain, Cuba and Chile amongst others. Exports also went out across the world to meet the growing demand for copper from new industries such as the railways and telegraph systems.

Apart from learning a little about this in school, living on the western side of the town away from what had largely become a scene of post-industrial dereliction
I was largely unaware of this during my early years.
In fact, the last copper works in Swansea only closed in 1980 although smelting had ended long before that.
Despite my relative ignorance, and I am not alone in this, my life was touched by influences from this industry. On our occasional train journeys in or out of the High St station I would see the moonscape that had been left by industry and from town you would see the bare hillside of Kilvey before the replanting in the 1960's of the Lower Swansea Valley

project. We visited an old army friend of my father's who lived near the aptly named Chemical Road. I naively thought it was named after a Chemists or possibly a chemistry set popular with children at that time.

Closer to home there were more positive influences. The Vivian family, John Vivian had founded the Hafod copper works in 1810 gave their name to Vivian road where the local library was, the Vivian arms pub in Sketty . The Vivian's employed the architect Henry Woodyer to design St Paul's church and the school opposite known now as the Stewart Hall and it was here that I went to Cubs and later the Scout troop who would regularly attend the church for church parades.

Singleton Park where I spent many hours in childhood was originally owned by the Vivians and bought by the town council as a public park in 1919. Much of it was developed by

Daniel Bliss who had trained at Kew Gardens. The lower part of the park now has Singleton Hospital and Swansea University with their administration housed in Singleton Abbey (built as Marino in1784) and bought by the Vivians in 1817. The previous photo shows the house in 1854.

Today the city has started to celebrate it's industrial history again with restoration works taking place at the Hafod-Morfa Copperworks site, Kilvey hill is green again and the river

Tawe has clean water with the river barrage has allowed river traffic and a marina.

I should also say that Swansea is a city and has been since 1969 but I always think of it as a town and still refer when going there as 'going into town.'
In common with other towns and cities during my lifetime there have been enormous social and physical changes in this time. Most of these changes are not unique to my town although some characteristics and past events of the location have influenced the changes. Nostalgia is a very strong human emotion and there is some kind of safety valve in the human memory that yearns for the good things in the past while subconsciously glossing over the negative aspects so that the past is often viewed through a rosy positive tint. It is quite common today for people to look at their cities and high streets and lament that traffic was never this bad, people were more smartly dressed and courteous and that good quality shopping could be found in all high streets. The same people will be families of multiple car ownership and would baulk at having to put on a collar and tie to go to a restaurant. The view is that this vibrant centre has been replaced by characterless chain stores with indifferent staff, often in bleak out of town retail parks and charity shops, nail bars and other non-essential retail has replaced useful shops in city centres.
In some ways I agree, in that I remember the town centre in the 1950's and 60's when parking was easy or buses were frequent and all shopping from a new school blazer to fresh food and a puppy or hamster could be found in the centre. People were smartly dressed but the baby boomer generation have only ourselves to blame for the decline in dress standards having eagerly discarded the collar and tie, embracing jeans and more relaxed leisure wear culminating in smart casual followed by 'very casual' judging by the lunch time exodus from offices.
This is not new and I am sure the Victorian generation were horrified by the 20th century.
My generations nostalgia for the vibrant city centre of the 1960's is only an echo of the previous generation who

enjoyed a bustling pre- war Swansea town centre. Quoting from the excellent 'Rebuilding Swansea 1941-1961 by Dinah Evans' published by West Glamorgan Archive Service:- An official survey in 1936 of the town identified a two acre covered market with over four hundred shops and stalls as well as 10 department stores, 51 multiple shops, 13 co-operative stores and almost a further three thousand individual shops covering the complete range of goods and services. Some of the facilities described in the Swansea stores pre-war would not have been out of place in Knightsbridge or New York.

They included a Viennese roof garden with sea views, a roof top track for petrol driven children's cars, full sized electric funfair style roundabout.

Ben Evans store had four storeys and included amongst their attractions a restaurant, a gentlemen's smoking room, a ladies' writing room and there were afternoon fashion shows to be watched while taking tea!

Possibly the most ambitious was in the pre-war David Evans store on Goat Street which in 1933 created an in-house Indian village. This was hosted by staff from the Indian sub-continent in traditional dress. The display included a carpet shop, an arts and crafts bazaar and a scale model of the Taj Mahal as well as a Temple, a Prayer room and an Indian theatre. The madness culminated in a Jungle room with scampering monkeys and a huge stuffed Bengal Tiger - these were certainly pre-political correctness days.

There is no mention of elephants so they must have realised that extravagance had its limits!

So nostalgia for past glories seems to be an entitlement for each generation. It remains to be seen if future generations will lament the passing of out of town malls, traffic jams and tattoo and nail parlours. Already the nostalgia exists for crowded, dirty, smokey pubs serving warm beer and not much else. Still this is meant to be an affectionate look back to my childhood so I had better tone this down. The truth is each generation's advances brings changes - some that are more welcome than others and it is always difficult to retain perspective when trying to achieve a balanced conclusion.

In some ways the city or town of Swansea has always suffered from an identity crisis. Is it a tourist centre on the fringe of the first designated Area of Outstanding Natural Beauty in the UK and if so why? Is there a dearth of decent hotel accommodation and no office of tourist information unlike any other decent tourist city? There is precious little recognition of the potential claim of the lower Swansea valley to be the seat of the Industrial Revolution with world wide trade and integrated metallurgy production in the late 17th and 18th centuries. It's focus as a regional shopping and trading centre from Victorian times has suffered in recent decades and the re-invention as a university city has certainly proved controversial in some quarters. The coming of containerisation in shipping has helped put the city docks into a decline with traffic a fraction today of what it was at it's peak. Maybe our geographical location which had such advantages for earlier developments is now proving an inherent disadvantage common to second cities in many other countries. There is the often heard lament of 'that will go to Cardiff' just forty miles up the road but forty miles closer to Westminster.

Recent developments in the city, as I must remember to call it, (it was made a city over fifty years ago!) have given me cause for optimism. Yes there is more traffic and the shops in the centre no longer supply all needs but we have internet shopping and out of town retail. Town centres everywhere are having to reinvent themselves and Swansea is no different. There are efforts by the city council to encourage much new development and these are to be celebrated. The number of students is a cause for celebration bringing diversity, youth and spending into the centre. Capitalising on the waterfront opportunities offered by the coast as well as the river and dock lands is another welcome development. The availability of brown field sites near the city centre allow new housing, leisure and service developments. The past is another place: you can't go back there so we must look to the future and embrace the changes. This location of a city by the sea has a lot to offer both now and in the future.

Postscript

This series of early life memories are being written at a time, to use an overused but appropriate phrase, of unprecedented challenges to the world through the 2020 global pandemic. My childhood years were characterised by a different set of fears usually relating to the outbreak of an armed conflict culminating in a world war. Given at the time of my birth it was just over five years since the second world war had been dramatically ended by the dropping of two atomic bombs by the Americans on the Japanese civilian populations of Hiroshima and Nagasaki with hundreds of thousands of deaths immediately and in the aftermath it is not surprising that this was a time of fear. The nations of the world were engaged in expensive military arms races and flashpoint had recently occurred in Korea, the Middle east and Eastern Europe. As I entered secondary school the Cuban missile brought the two great powers of that time to the brink of nuclear conflict. Thankfully it was averted. The fear of nuclear war was replaced on the brink of my teenage years by anxieties over the eleven plus and whether I would go to the same school as my friends. The fears were to prove groundless but that all came later.

Unfortunately, the pandemic of the last eighteen months was not averted and for all of us this period has seen our lives changed in ways that would have been thought to have been a science fiction film script. Fortunately the more extreme scenarios of looting and food riots appear to have been largely avoided. Interesting that lockdowns in the USA provoked a rush to buy firearms whilst in this country there was a rush on toilet paper shortages. It's difficult to work out who was the most frightened by the crisis!

All of that apart it has been a strange year and for my own part I want to record the impact of the pandemic on my life much of it, no doubt, trivial.

Firstly, although the media had carried stories of a virus in China since early in 2020 we had spent Christmas on holiday in Lisbon and been away seeing friends in Sussex and later in mid-wales in January. We had a week booked for the beginning of March in a hotel in the Algarve and at the time

of the holiday saw no reason to cancel it. Some six weeks or so later we expected to travel to the Greek island of Crete to our little holiday home there where we usually spent a few weeks each spring and autumn.
The day we flew to Portugal the UK had only announced three covid related deaths of people returning to the country with links to outbreaks abroad. The first death was announced four days before we flew. That week the Cheltenham Festival took place normally with over a quarter of a million people mixing freely. It has since been described as a 'super-spreader' event. In Liverpool 3000 Spanish fans flew in for the Liverpool vs Athletico Madrid cup. tie. In Portugal and at the airports all seems normal with no masks sight and in the hotel we were the only people we saw using hand sanitiser but given we were all helping ourselves to hot and cold food from buffet dishes this was probably ineffective. Media coverage on the TV news escalated during the week with alarming footage of hospital scenes in Italy and Spain as well as the situation in Wuhan, China.

We arrived back into the UK on the night of 13/14th March with the announcements that the FA were suspending the premier league season, local elections were postponed and after the first UK hospital announced a critical emergency due to being overwhelmed by covid cases. It started to feel a different world to the one we had left on holiday. Within days the closure of non-essential shops, pubs and restaurants were announced and in short order more restrictions were announced. Working from home, travel restrictions, only one hour's outside exercise near home and facemasks etc. The immediate priority was food deliveries. We had been having deliveries at home for some time from one of the supermarkets but despite being a regular customer no slots were available so not wishing to mix inside I scouted online for some click and collect slots from any supermarket and luckily booked one for later that week. Other measures and the daily Downing Street bad news press conferences are familiar to many of us so I won't cover that here. Our own lives closed down, no visitors to the house, an hour's exercise a day outside, keeping our distance from strangers and neighbours alike. Shopping on-line for everything. The Zoom videoconferencing app becoming a way of seeing others. The spraying of post and parcels and vigorous washing of hands, the fear of going to hospital if any other health issue arose. The hearing about a few friends and acquaintances being tested for covid. The country grinding to a halt and the news channels being dominated by this one story and life closing down.

We were fortunate as our lives were less affected then for many others. The deaths and illnesses of loved ones, the isolation for many people, the occurrence of 'long Covid' illnesses. The impact on education, careers and livelihoods were terrible for many - it affected everyone to greater or lesser extents.

Life is now different - the brief and nervous respite of the summer and tentative outings and brief stays in covid secure hotels in Wales before the second lockdown and a very isolated Christmas and the aftermath. The relief of vaccinations recently hasn't given me enough confidence to regularly go back into supermarkets yet. Writing this reminds me of a childhood anecdote often repeated by my Mum who answered the door one day to a boy living down the road from us. His opening comment was a little mystifying to her -

"Can I see them?"
-'Pardon?' answered Mum.
"The chickens - I've come to see Geoff's chickens"
-'What chickens?'
"I've heard Geoff has Chickens - in a Box!"
I was in bed upstairs - with chickenpox - mystery solved.

Living in Wales with some of the powers and regulations devolved we frequently found ourselves shouting at the radio or TV - "IN ENGLAND!" When national restrictions were announced but this only added another layer of confusion to what and where and when we could do things. We felt fortunate to have travelled so frequently in previous years but in some senses it made us feel the loss of freedom more acutely. We knew we were lucky not to have the worry of careers or more elderly parents in care homes. We were also aware we were now because of age and some pre existing health conditions that we were in the vulnerable and at risk category. Like many of our contemporaries we hunkered down.

End piece

I'd like to end on a positive note so I have captioned some photos that are too good not to use.
I also give thanks to my parents Joan and Llew for my happy upbringing and to my wife for her enthusiastic support in my writing and most of all being here with me in the present.

My grandfather providing inspiration for 'Madness' with his trousers.

My Mum rehearsing her Shirley Temple kitten juggling act.

Here I am providing future employment for osteopaths and dentists.

My attempt to join a fledgling punk band by playing the Duck.

My Grannie's Parrot sketch

Printed in Dunstable, United Kingdom